*I am a man with a heart that offends
with its lonely and greedy demands*
—SUFJAN STEVENS

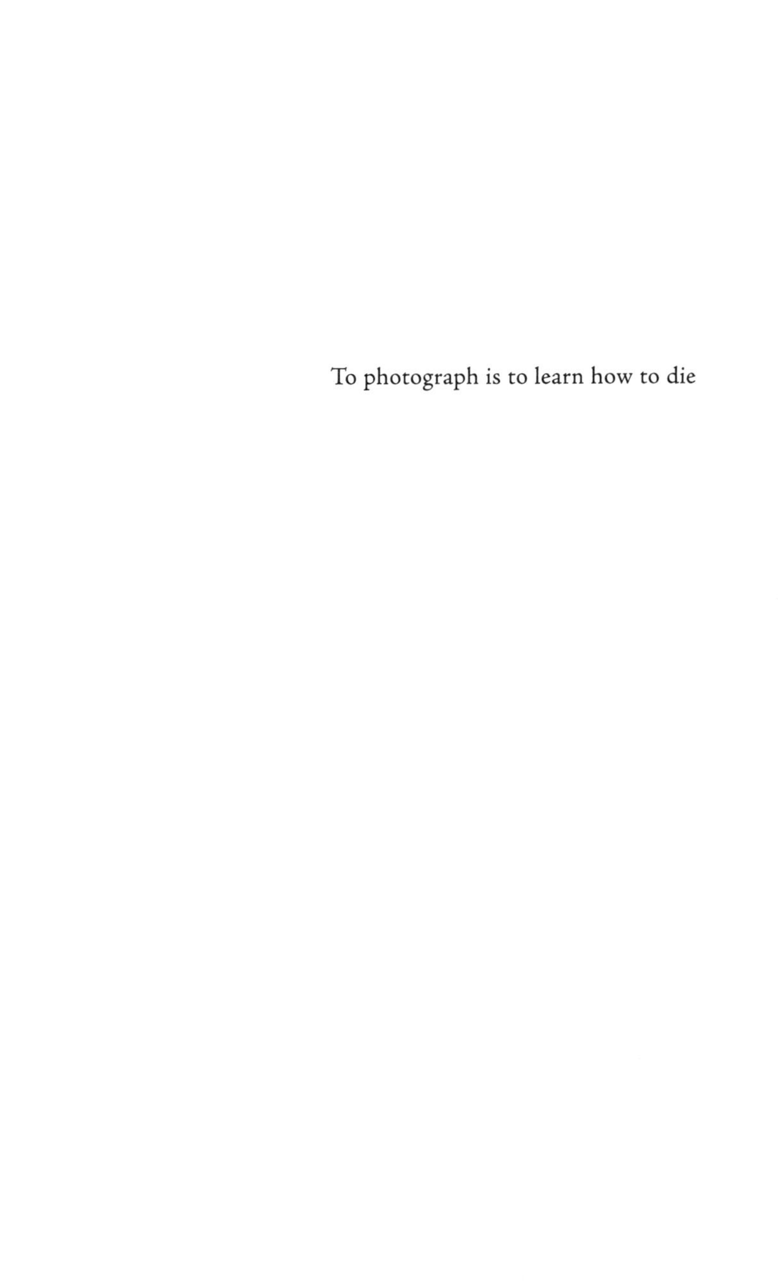

To photograph is to learn how to die

THE ICE PLANT ✦ LOS ANGELES ✦ 2022

Tim Carpenter

TO PHOTOGRAPH IS TO LEARN HOW TO DIE

an essay with digressions

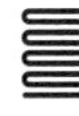

PREAMBLE

> You are here, and later on you will no longer be here, and you know it. *What is not* corresponds in your mind to *what is*. This is because the power over you of *what is* produces the power in you of *what is not*; and the latter power changes into a feeling of impotence upon contact with *what is*. So we revolt against facts; we cannot admit a fact like death. Our hopes, our grudges, all this is a direct, instantaneous product of the conflict between *what is* and *what is not*.
> —PAUL VALÉRY

I am writing in the early 2020s. The thoughts of many people are properly engaged with the historical and the topical—with politics and ideologies and the like. With *events*. My head is there, too, but the constant pressure of the external in these years has, perhaps unsurprisingly, also led me more fully into the equally stormy internal. "It is a violence from within that protects us from a violence without," Wallace Stevens wrote. The human imagination has "something to do with our self-preservation" and "helps us to live our lives."

Preserving the self has meant, in my case, making photographs (lots of them) in a conscious attempt to reconcile the conflict between *what is* and *what is not*. This vocation has shown me that such reconciliations—to the extent they are even achievable—could never have just happened in my head. What I seem to require instead is the friction of the materially circumscribed activity of photography: an activity that uniquely entangles the actual and the imaginary, and which results in a beguilingly inscrutable product: a new thing in the world that *is itself* a conditional accord between what is given in the real and what is possible in the mind.

"How shall we learn what it is our hearts believe in?" Archibald MacLeish once asked. For me the answer is working with and through the camera—a peculiar machine that is the most plainly useful thing I will ever encounter. Which makes me curious about the nature of the desire to make things in this way.

As a foundation, I have to believe that all people know the ache of the conundrum described by Valéry. Yet obviously only some of us—a small handful, really—are compelled to make something of it: an aesthetic object in which a specific instance of felt life is evoked by the distillation of *what is* as subject matter and *what is not* as form. Of course, these two essential aspects of any particular picture or poem are inextricable as experienced by the viewer or reader. But in our activity as makers, we gauge subject matter and form as distinct facets of the whole, in order to shape with discipline and purpose. Such was the explicit effort of Stevens, who, over a long career, pondered the individual imagination as a creative (and, notably: *de*creative) faculty that could in various ways manage (but never resolve) the tension between *what is* and *what is not*—an active capacity consequential both in poems and in life.

If your goal is to make significant, enduring things, then, as far as I can tell, the whole deal resides in the quite rigorous use of your imaginative gift to get at the ineffable (*what is not*), rather than to portray what is already effable. Beware, though: because of our fundamental limitations, the aesthetic object—your work—will necessarily fail both the possibilities of your mind and the givenness of the world; I hope to persuade you not only that this is okay, but that one's humanity depends upon these near-misses.

Given all that, it's easy to see that 'the ineffable' and 'the self' are, for my purposes, synonymous. But what I'd like to suggest (by working backward from the aesthetic object) goes further: that 'form' and 'self' are pretty much identical as well. We are nothing but form-making creatures, each of us a one-off, perpetually knitting inner to outer (while simultaneously unraveling it all) to fashion a kind of idiosyncratic day-to-day, hour-to-hour livability of our given lot. Which then somehow over time becomes a singular personhood. (You might notice that, by analogy, 'self' equates with *what is not*, and so we'll need to talk about that, too.)

Shifting our attention outside: the stuff of reality is stubborn, recalcitrant. It will never meet us in the ways we might wish. Thus Valéry's revolt against facts. Fortunately, blessedly, we do have moments of vivid experience when interior and exterior come into a sort of tentative alignment, as if they're neurons between which a synapse has miraculously fired. Calling these 'epiphanies,' we rejoice in the mere suspicion of transcendence.

And, inevitably, we despair: the ephemerality of these revelations is a painful echo of our own mortality. Yet, strangely, it is this great brokenness of self that compels some of us to make an object out of such a moment — not a thing that is 'about,' as in recollection, but rather something that is the very cry of its occasion, "the poem as it is, / Not as it was," as Stevens would have it.

To do this, we find ways to short-circuit the cognitive feedback loop — the ceaseless calibration of the inexhaustible need within and the unrelenting resistance without — to arrest the existential frustration, if only for an instant. To adapt Iris Murdoch's formulation, we 'unself.' This is Montaigne, earlier than Murdoch, on that topic:

> Cicero says that philosophizing is nothing other than getting ready to die. That is because study and contemplation draw our souls somewhat outside ourselves, keeping them occupied away from the body, a state which both resembles death and which forms a kind of apprenticeship for it; or perhaps because all the wisdom and argument in the world eventually comes down to one conclusion; which is to teach us not to be afraid of dying.

I believe that using a camera can draw us away from our selves. That it is a meaningfully constrained way of thinking and knowing that enables us to conjure relationships among otherwise uncooperative earthly things; new and valuable correspondences which never actually existed. That these novel sets of relationships—called 'photographs'—are useful because of the independent authority they possess to both defy and embrace impermanence and to convey to other human beings the essence of a separate self's fleeting and often furtive connections with the obstinate thusness of it all. In short, that such pictures can get us about as close to the ineffable as our mortal shortcomings will allow.

And what's more: working with the camera has the warrant to turn this whole fearful mess on its head: to demonstrate that humility in the face of the actual and the transient has the paradoxical power to effect a true and earned freedom. That it authorizes ultimately the affirmation of life, the final yes.

This is what I want to tell you: to photograph is to learn how to die.

ABOUT THE TEXT

This book consists of an essay in four parts; the primary thread of its argument is in the same black type you're reading now. You could follow only this channel of thought and get pretty much the entirety of the case I want to make. †

[Within the main text you'll find brief, and sometimes not-so-brief, asides—treated like so—that clarify terms and add context. These are still part of the core claim, and essential to its understanding.]

†   Detouring from the central subject are a number of digressions (in blue type) that match to specific points along the way, often to expand or enliven, occasionally to delimit or contradict, sometimes to depart and explore. These are often standalone in nature, entire essays unto themselves.

Along the way you'll encounter other voices (in orange type), irreducible insights without which this book would not exist.

You could return to the stuff in blue and orange after reading the core theme, or take the slow road

‡   I wonder, though: Isn't that the main (or only) reason to quote something — to have it relate to the circumstances of quotation? Anyway, the Danto is from a pretty good book called *The Transfiguration of the Commonplace*, in which he says something else that I find significant (and also quotable): "People do not ordinarily say that they believe X; they simply act as though X were true, and hence as though the world were that way. Thus we refer to our practices of the world rather than to our beliefs, and feel as though it is reality itself we are describing rather than ourselves we are confessing." As you'll see, all of this is highly relevant to the task at hand.

and digest it all in sequence. I suggest the latter approach, but it's up to you.

Some things to keep in mind:

1. Throughout, I'll talk about *what is not* and *what is*, using pairs of words like 'the unreal and the real,' or 'mind and world.' Don't get hung up on the strict definitions or philosophical implications of these terms (there is much disagreement among the professionals, anyway); just remember that all I'm ever talking about is the basic dichotomy between your self and all that is not your self.

2. I've adopted a convention to talk about the fundamental aspects of a photograph (and of all aesthetic objects). 'Subject matter' means the things that were in front of the lens. Everything else is 'form.' The 'content' of a picture is its totality: the combination of subject matter and form.

3. It feels lucky to have you here.

I

SONNET ISOLATE

There's what's inside you and there's what's outside you. That's all there is.

We call the interior the 'self' or the 'mind.' The exterior we call the 'not-self' or the 'world.'

This dichotomy can feel somewhat artificial, of course, because we are so entirely entangled with the world. Our bodies and brains are made of the same stuff as everything else, after all.

And yet, at some point, we began to experience the self and the not-self as distinct.

In other words, we gained consciousness.

We acquired imagination: the capacity to ponder *what is not.* We were no longer bound entirely by any actual state of affairs, by *what is.* The possible gained equal footing with the given; absences and expectations were born—and with them came longing. And as we made space for the unreal, a previously unknown mode of thought, we isolated the *self* from all that is not the self.

To be sure: not everyone was (or *is,* for that matter) pleased with this state of affairs. Ralph Waldo Emerson wrote: "It is very unhappy, but too late to be helped, the discovery we have made that we exist. The discovery is called the Fall of Man." 1

Why so sorrowful? Some foundational shift occurred in the human brain, and we came to know ourselves

1   Emerson was not, on balance, all that sad about existing.

as our selves, as somehow separate from the world.
But why call that our *fall* and not our *rise*?

> The force behind the movement of time is a mourn-
> ing that will not be comforted. That is why the first
> event is known to have been an expulsion, and the
> last is hoped to be a reconciliation and return.
> —MARILYNNE ROBINSON (MR)

Because the truth hurts: The world is chaotic and
utterly indifferent to the self. The not-self is incon-
stant and without meaning.

> From this the poem springs: that we live in a place
> That is not our own and, much more, not ourselves
> —WS

Nor can we rely on the self—it is *truly* unreal, nothing
but an incalculable tumult of neural activity, pitched
and patched together, a chimera of the brain. 2

2   "Selfhood in humans is not the expression of
any central unity. It is a pattern of organisation," John
Gray writes. "Our perceptions are fragments, picked
out from an unfathomable richness—but there is no
one doing the selecting... We are programmed to perceive identity in ourselves, when in truth there is only
change. We are hardwired for the illusion of self."
I believe this entirely, and yet I'm fine with the

Plus: it's got an expiration date. A hard stop. And we know it, painfully. Simone Weil spoke of "the possibility of death that lies locked up in each moment."

> Nothing is left us now but death. We look at it with a grim satisfaction, saying, "There at least is reality that will not dodge us."
> —RALPH WALDO EMERSON (RWE)

We deal with these profound limitations in one of two significant ways: 1) by claiming that the dichotomy we perceive between mind and world is a false one, perhaps even asserting that there's some external force that underlies and coheres (and even

deception. For, as Wallace Stevens writes: "The world about us would be desolate except for the world within us." My interest, like Marilynne Robinson's in many of her essays, is in "reauthorizing experience, felt reality, as one important testimony to the nature of reality itself."

If I didn't put full stock in the real as felt, there would be no reason to write this book. Or to make photographs or do much of anything else beyond staying alive. But to be clear: the meaning to be made from human experience is the extent of what I'm talking about here; at no point will this be about the 'soul.' The self, entirely an assemblage of the brain, ceases to exist when the body dies. And this is immortalizes) the self and all of creation; or 2) by accepting the fundamental ache, and employing internal human faculties to create significance and affirm the value of our finite lives.

This book exists because I choose the latter. I believe there is always and forever a divide between the acutely limited and wanting self and the infinite and purposeless not-self, and this (the "dumbfoundering abyss" according to Stevens) is all we have to work with. As Keith Ansell Pearson says, "We are creatures of sense and meaning who dwell in a universe devoid of sense and meaning."

important: it's only because of this finitude that anything really matters at all.

Materialism of mind makes some people uncomfortable; many reject it outright. "We can't be just hunks of meat," they say. But that's what we are: hunks of meat whose creations include *Don Quixote* and "The Rite of Spring" and *To the Lighthouse* and *Purple Rain*. I'm sure you can think of others.

Materialism does not imply determinism. I'm convinced (though easily, because I'm way over my head in this area) that quantum indeterminacy and other theories of matter blow a hole in the idea of strict causation. I love these notes sent by Jean Paulhan to Stevens: "It is admitted, since Planck,

This deliberate choice, I think, is everything. Although the desire for preternatural comfort may seem benign, such consolation is nonetheless a delusion. And if we deceive ourselves by longing for (and believing in) invented worlds, we are also bound to misrepresent the world we actually inhabit.

that determinism—the relation of cause to effect exists, or so it seems, on the human scale, only by means of an aggregate of statistical compensations and as the physicists say, by virtue of macroscopic approximations. (There is much to dream about in these macroscopic approximations.) As to the true nature of corpuscular or quantic phenomenon, well, try to imagine them. No one has yet succeeded. But the poet—it is possible."

In any case, the point here is not to convey unassailable truths, primarily because I reject such thing(s). Rather, my aim is to be very serious about the real and profound limitations of the self, while celebrating the hell out of its felt conjoinings with the not-self, and all that can be made thereof: to dream—and to dwell—in macroscopic approximations. I believe, to rephrase Paulhan, that for "the photographer—it is possible."

Because we must rely entirely on internal capacities to generate meaning, our selves are basically the sum of the ever-changing relationships between mind and world. Our challenge is to observe and know these representations—without delusion—even if this scrutiny necessarily reopens the tender underlying wound. 3

3   Finding no inherent meaning in the cosmos is of course a basic definition of nihilism—a discomfiting word for many. Yet I accept no teleological explanations of being, and no ultimate truth (or falseness). We are not haplessly misperceiving some underlying unity; everything is simply random and impermanent.

And yet there is immeasurable worth in our existence. That's one of the big lessons from Friedrich Nietzsche: whereas his predecessors (and many others who would follow) saw nothing but absolute despair and degradation in the rejection of supernatural or universal principles, he saw an opportunity to enthusiastically search for natural—human—standards of consequence and merit: "There are no moral phenomena at all, only a moral interpretation of phenomena." The key point being that meaning and purpose are not things external to us, but rather values that are wholly internally generated, whenever mind meets world. Thus they are of consequence to us only insofar as they are useful—beneficial to actual lived lives. Robert Solomon says of Nietzsche's nihilism that "it is a 'destructive' philosophy, as so often is

"Was it Boscovich who found out that bodies never come in contact?" Emerson asked. "Well, souls never touch their objects. An innavigable sea washes with silent waves between us and the things we aim at and converse with."

Yet, somehow, across the innavigable, *what is* and *what is not* do achieve momentary alignment in what we call 'thought.'

Now, whatever is sensation is essentially *present.* There is no other definition of the present except sensation itself, which includes, perhaps, the impulse to action that would modify that sensation. On the other hand, whatever is properly thought, image, sentiment, is always, in some way, *a production of*

charged, only in the sense that one destroys a field of weeds to plant a garden."

"That human life has no external point or *telos* is a view as difficult to argue as its opposite, and I shall simply assert it," writes Iris Murdoch, "I can see no evidence to suggest that human life is not something self-contained... Our destiny can be examined but it cannot be justified or totally explained. We are simply here. And if there is any kind of sense or unity in human life, and the dream of this does not cease to haunt us, it is of some other kind and must be sought within a human experience which has nothing outside it."

absent things. Memory is the substance of all thought. Anticipation and its gropings, desire, planning, the projection of our hopes, our fears, are the main interior activity of our being.

Thought is, in short, the activity which causes what does not exist to come alive in us, lending to it, whether we will or no, our present powers, making us take the part for the whole, the image for reality, and giving us the illusion of seeing, acting, suffering, and possessing independently of our dear old body...

—PAUL VALÉRY (PV)

Although mind and world are not and cannot be unified, we can (we *do*, because there is no other choice) work within these constraints to bring what's inside and what's outside into a useful, workable— sometimes even amicable—accord. 4

4   Without constraints, no genuine accord.
At first, I understood the term 'solipsism' only in its most extreme meaning: that the solipsist believes that nothing exists outside of mind (i.e., everything is a projection). And it's confusing when you're young, because that seems patently ridiculous but maybe also non-refutable? The only thing I could think was, "If

Strangely enough, the imagination that is responsible for the existential breach is the *very same faculty* that perpetually acts to align the self with the not-self, creating vital and valuable relationships— between inside and out—that didn't exist before.

[I will use the words 'imagination' and 'imaginative' quite a lot here, so it's crucial to be clear early on as to what they mean in this context.

"We use our imagination not to escape the world but to join it," says Iris Murdoch. The imagination is not make-believe or fantasy untethered to the actual world;

I really am making all this up, why aren't I doing a much better job of it? Like, why would I *invent* Brad Pitt without *being* him?"

Turns out that line of inquiry is not so far off. Here's Isaiah Berlin, relating the thoughts of Johann Gottlieb Fichte: "You become aware of the self only when there is some kind of resistance... It is the impact of the obstacle upon you which makes you aware of your self as an entity different from the not-self which you are trying to understand, or to feel, or perhaps to dominate, conquer, alter, mould—at any rate do something to or at... In the resistance emerged the self and the not-self. Without the not-self, no sense of the self. Without the sense of the

this is the most important thing to accept, whether in pondering ordinary day-to-day experience or contemplating the profoundest aesthetic objects.

> I'm always highly irritated by people who imply that writing fiction is an escape from reality. It is a plunge into reality and it's very shocking to the system.
> —FLANNERY O'CONNOR (FO'C)

Samuel Taylor Coleridge (and seemingly everyone who addresses this issue refers back to Coleridge) laid down the law way back when by distinguishing 'imagination' from 'fancy,' which "has no other counters to play with, but fixities and definites" and so "must receive

self, no sense of the not-self."

This is important because it not only dismisses the worrisome aspects of solipsism to my satisfaction, it also makes clear the need for discord between the self and not-self for either to even be realized.

The recalcitrance of the actual, and what this recalcitrance implies for both fleeting everyday life and durable authentic artworks, underlies much of what I have to say. And on the practical level of thinking about the products of the mind, I became more comfortable with the idea of solipsism when I saw how easily Harold Bloom used the term in his criticism; he simply assumed its presence in some degree in all art.

*all its materials ready made from the law of associa-
tion." Meaning: the fanciful maker merely chooses and
places, without creating new, dynamic (i.e., formal)
associations that transform subject matter.*

*It's worth quoting Wendell Berry at length here: "The
term 'imagination' in what I take to be its truest sense
refers to a mental faculty that some people have used
and thought about with the utmost seriousness. The
sense of the verb 'to imagine' contains the full richness of
the verb 'to see.' To imagine is to see most clearly, famil-
iarly, and understandingly with the eyes, but also to see
inwardly, with 'the mind's eye.' It is to see, not passively,
but with a force of vision and even with visionary force.
To take it seriously we must give up at once any notion
that imagination is disconnected from reality or truth or
knowledge. It has nothing to do either with clever imi-
tation of appearances or with 'dreaming up.' It does not
depend upon one's attitude or point of view, but grasps
securely the qualities of things seen or envisioned... I will*

So let's accept a basic level of spirited solipsism in
all of the meetings of mind and world, because that's
just the way it works. But let's also place heavy emphasis on the primacy of the actual, particularly when it
comes to the creation of aesthetic objects.

say, from my own belief and experience, that imagination thrives on contact, on tangible connection."

My only quibble with Berry: one's imaginative approach does indeed relate to one's attitude or point of view. That's why everyone's is different, and why any one individual's approach changes from day to day or even from moment to moment. Valéry nailed this, beguilingly: "Understanding is a closed thing. To understand A is to be able to reconstruct A. And to imagine is only to understand oneself."

But Berry is right in calling the imagination a 'faculty.' It is not synonymous with the self, but is rather an instrument of the self that thrives on—and draws its raw material from—its connection with the actual.] 5

Coleridge divided the imagination into the 'primary' and the 'secondary.' The former is "the living

5   There's more to know about the concept of the imagination in Stevens specifically, and I'm going to belabor this point because it relates so wholly to how I've approached the issue at hand. "He is under a necessity set by a pair of indubitable facts—that he is in reality, and that his imagination inevitably transforms it," says Roy Harvey Pearce of Stevens. This is

power and prime agent of *all* human perception"
(emphasis mine). Daily life—moment-to-moment
existence—consists of an incessant, and mostly
involuntary, imaginative tending to the rapport
between internal and external, and the bulk of this
responsive activity is on a minor scale, barely or
maybe not even conscious (i.e., "There's a curb, lift
your foot").

crucial because it's also uniquely and precisely the
necessity of the photographer in the world. (There
is much more to come about the particulars of this
necessity.)

"The acute intelligence of the imagination," Stevens writes, "the illimitable resources of its memory,
its power to possess the moment it perceives—if
we were speaking of light itself, and thinking of the
relationship between objects and light, no further
demonstration would be necessary. Like light, it adds
nothing, except itself... To be at the end of fact is not
to be at the beginning of imagination but it is to be at
the end of both. The poet must get rid of the hieratic
in everything that concerns him and must move constantly in the direction of the credible."

The credible is the believable—which is not the
same as absolute fact, but rather that which puts us
in "agreement with reality." It's like a lowest common
denominator: that which all people can reasonably
rely upon in daily life (and revel in with art). The

The secondary imagination is the province of the artist. It "dissolves, diffuses, dissipates, in order to recreate: or where this process is rendered impossible, yet still at all events it struggles to idealize and to unify. It is essentially vital, even as all objects (as objects) are essentially fixed and dead."

That struggle is our focus here: the act of (de)creation; the use of the imagination, in its special sense

of *poesis*—the making (and unmaking) of significant and useful (albeit provisional) correspondences
between subject and object. 6

We must also consider the occasional external
manifestation of those internal mental representations. Because, to clarify: *poesis* is not a 'poem.' The
former is the perpetual meaning-making activity of
all people; the latter is a thing made by only a few,
every now and again. The shared root, however,

> realizing in esthetic form certain epistemological,
> ontological, and moral propositions. The relation-
> ship between the propositions and the poetry is this:
> that esthetic experience is the only means we have of
> initiating the inquiry by which we arrive at those prop-
> ositions, and is, moreover, the only means we have of
> realizing and believing in them... So the poet-esthete
> becomes the philosopher-moralist."
> As for the 'poet-esthete,' so for the photographer.

6   There is always an ethical element to the construction of these representations: "As soon as we
see a new image," Nietzsche says, "we immediately
construct it with the aid of all our previous experiences, depending on the degree of our honesty and
justice. All experiences are moral experiences, even in
the realm of sense perception."

makes clear the way in which aesthetic objects (as products of imagination) function in relation to lived lives, *for both the makers and the consumers* of those objects.

The essential *usefulness* of that interaction—between art and person—is a central theme of this book. (My idea of usefulness is closely related to Nietzsche's concept of *value* in human life. It doesn't matter whether an ideal is 'true' or 'false'—because nothing is ultimately true or false anyway—but rather whether it contributes to human flourishing. If it does so contribute, then it's useful.)

Aesthetic objects are useful in that they are the best (maybe the only) way to make unique maps of our selves, to get us achingly close to the ineffable, and to communicate our tentative findings to others. (This topic will be the focus of Part II.)

The contents of our selves are, by their very nature, inexpressible. There is no actual entity to be described; it's nothing but a tangled thicket of complementary and contradictory imagined relationships of mind and world. Because both the internal and the external are always changing, our multiform representations are also in constant short- and long-term flux.

My concern: how we gauge that flux, how we map and manifest the entirely conditional expanse between *what is* and *what is not.*

Sometimes the gap seems despairingly immense; at other times it narrows such that we have a brief sense of real connection.

But the abyss abides. And because its opposing banks are permanently unstable, our gauging is without cease.

In the short term, we might call this calibration a mood or an attitude. Considered over longer periods, it is our posture or perspective vis-à-vis the constraints of the world, which is to say it is essentially *who we are.*

> We would think ourselves continuous with the world if
>   we did not have moods.
> It is state-of-mind that discloses to us
> (Heidegger claims) that we are beings that have been
>   thrown into something else.
> —ANNE CARSON (AC)

Which is not to imply solidity. Our selves are always and necessarily provisional. (Keep this in mind; it will pertain later, in the consideration of photographs.)

The flux we experience both within and without is manageable to some degree, but it seems to thwart our intentions at every turn. Our inability to master this contingency causes us great pain.

Happily—and this is important—human agency is possible in all of this, because we can (we already do, often) take an active role in our *observations* of the ongoing calibrations that occur in the imaginative space that is the self. (This willful appraisal from a position of remove is what it means to inhabit the 'Supreme Fiction' of Wallace Stevens, as we shall see.)

> I am at risk of another kind of dualist thinking, representing my mind as a rather autonomous being in its own right, which now and then asserts its notions and preoccupations, obliging me to collaborate in realizing them. My mind and I. Since I have set about the project of reauthorizing experience, I can only report that the dichotomy sometimes feels this absolute.
>
> —MR

It is this vigorous scrutiny of one's self and of the modulations of one's self—and also a cultivation of this process of self-examination—that underlies what I've come to see as a fruitful means of not only making useful aesthetic objects, but also of living a life that is affirmative despite our limitations, a life that might afford one a significant freedom.

This approach is the recognition and management of a couple of interrelated processes that have (a bit confusingly) both come to be known as *decreation*. Because each process has a role in how I regard the correlation of everyday experience to art (and to photographs in particular) it's important to distinguish and define them here.

...

The first of these decreative activities—let's call it 'forgetting'—occurs when old relationships between self and not-self are abandoned or modified so that new connections will have room to thrive. This culling of the inconsequential is essential to the creation of any aesthetic object; it will be examined in Part II.

We'll keep the word 'decreation' for the second aspect of this process, in which the 'created' world of projected human meanings is 'decreated' by the determined diminishment or elimination of those projections. I've found that in this sense it's closely related to the workings of the camera, and so will be fully explored in Part III.

For now, the crucial point is that the constant alignment of self—as we calibrate interior and exterior worlds against one another—necessarily entails an equally constant de-alignment and re-alignment of that which came before.

Throughout our lives—as we grow and change, gain and lose, create and destroy, forget and remember—we fashion a more or less stable union between the internal and the external, and we say that we are bringing *form* to bear on the situation.

> We fling ourselves, constantly longing, on this form.
> —ws

[This form-making process is essential, not only to short- and long-term mental life but also to the making of any sort of aesthetic object, as we'll discuss in Part II.]

Such is the unceasing activity of us humans, inclined as we are to find stability (however tentative), and a resultant predictability (however rough), as useful to living, in respects ranging from the mundane to the grand. 7

7   For a few years a while back, I saw a guy who was deeply closeted; he was Russian and worked and lived with Russians out in Brighton Beach, and a boyfriend was not a possibility for him. Tima was on the quiet side of reticent, more due to his personality than to any lack of facility with English. One night, out of the blue, he said, "I feel different when I'm here."

I thought about this a lot then and have considerably more since; it's one of only a few insights he ever allowed me.

He was saying that, when we were together, what he wanted and what he could have were aligned in a way that was otherwise unattainable. (I like to think he was telling me something else too...) I could ponder, and (as I'm doing now) write about, the concept of 'formal coherence' for ever and ever, but it'd be just

Form-making is embodied in abstraction.

An abstraction is not the thing in itself; it is, rather, a meeting of mind and thing(s). We cannot know things in and of themselves because we cannot get

that—a concept—without Tima gently knocking the wind out of me.

There's a Wilco song called "I am trying to break your heart." I once used that phrase as the title of my online dating profile, to signify my favorite band and also I figured if someone got the reference he'd also get me. (Note: a few dudes wrote that they were appalled by the sentiment.) Because the deal here is: for a heart to be broken, it first has to be made complete by a meeting of the ideal and the real, by a requiting of yearning and its object: imagination fulfilled. (This is cyclical, of course; "For nothing can be sole or whole / That has not been rent," as W.B. Yeats would have it.)

Eventually, Tima had to go back home. I knew this would happen all along, and more importantly I knew that he would never be mine, so it had always been easy to consider the entire thing as having no strings attached. Except that when he did go, I suddenly realized that I didn't want him to. I was mad at myself for the longing, and also doubly upset for not having seen it coming. As if through inattentiveness to my self, I'd mismanaged a situation that could have been controlled.

Formal coherence became, for me, just a concept once again. For many months, almost a year, when I

out of our own way. But we can try, and there is
great value in the attempt—this gets at the second
sense of decreation (a subject of Part III).

made pictures I couldn't seem to get the world to cor-
respond to my heart or my head. Imagination failed
me entirely. Or maybe it transmuted somehow, because
eventually a handful of those photographs were made
into a book that I'm proud of chiefly because it is wholly
adequate to its impetus. And I was grateful, relieved,
when at the end of this time I read Helen Vendler on
Stevens (an end perhaps hastened by these words):

"Since feeling—to use Wordsworthian terms—
is the organizing principle of poetry (both narratively,
insofar as poetry is a history of feeling, and structur-
ally, insofar as poetry is a science or analysis of feeling),
without feeling the world of the poet is a chaos. As
we know, as the poet knows, the absence of feeling is
itself—since the poet is still alive—a mask for feelings
too powerful to make themselves felt: these manifest
themselves in this poem ["Chaos in Motion and Not in
Motion"] as that paradoxical 'desire without an object
of desire,' libido unfocused and therefore churning in
all directions—like a wind, as the last line of the poem
says, 'that lashes at everything at once.' Unfocused and
chaotic libido does not provide a channel along which

An abstraction is necessarily a fiction—but this word should not trouble us, because 'fiction' in this sense does not imply truth or untruth. 8

> Only fiction will accommodate the facts of life... Our choice, in so far as we have one, is not between fiction and fact, but between good and bad fiction... If it's a matter of words, if it's a function of language, if it's concerned with what it's like or not like to be human, it will prove to be some sort of fiction.
> —WRIGHT MORRIS (WM)

thought can move. Once there is an object of desire, the mind can exert all its familiar diversions—decoration, analysis, speculation, fantasy, drama, and so on. But with no beloved object, the mind is at a loss; the hero of the poem has 'lost the whole in which he was contained... / He knows he has nothing more to think about.' The landscape is the objective correlative to this state of mind: 'There is lightning and the thickest thunder.'"

8 This is not a new problem; my understanding is that Plato denounced poetry and painting because he considered them to be imitations of life—merely mimetic—and thus false not only to this world but also to what he thought of as the eternal forms of an underlying metaphysical order. (Moreover, he feared the obvious popular power of these inventions.) Aristotle set things right by removing the aesthetic object from a direct correlation with reality, asserting fiction where Plato saw falsehood.

Using a word made of the letters t-r-e-e to indicate what we all know to be a tree, for example, is an abstraction. It is a fiction. And yet, in everyday usage, no one would consider this a falsehood. We might even say that it shows fidelity to the real world. That it is 'objective.'

> The aim of what we properly call objectivity is the fullest possible recognition of the integral and entire existence of the object... In the face of the certainty that the effort of objectivity will fall short of what it aims at, those who undertake to make the effort do so out of something like a sense of intellectual honor and out of good faith that in the practical life, which includes the moral life, some good must follow from even the relative success of the endeavor.
>
> The line between a truly passionate naturalism and an extravagant fantasy is always a thin one. *The obsessive contemplation of the objectivity of objects, the thingishness of things, is a step toward surrealism, perhaps towards madness.* (emphasis mine—let's not get carried away)
> —LIONEL TRILLING (LT)

There are of course other fictions—many enjoyable ones—that are less objective, or even outlandish. Again, we should not worry: the weighing and judging of these human inventions is not just unavoidable, it's one of our most thrilling pursuits.

Lionel Trilling wrote that "To know a story when we see one, to know it for a story, to know that it is not reality itself but that it has clear and effective relations with reality—this is one of the great disciplines of the mind." This statement is a pretty decent entry point to the gist of the Stevens poem that inspired much of my thinking in this book: "Notes Toward a Supreme Fiction." It's a long poem, and it's been analyzed by the best. Fortunately for you, exegesis is not my aim here; but the poem does provide an infrastructure for this whole thing (i.e., "Poetry sometimes crowns the search for happiness. It is itself a search for happiness"), and since I'll refer to its themes many times over, here's the lay of the land.

The poem consists of three parallel sections: "It Must Be Abstract," "It Must Change," and "It Must Give Pleasure." With regard to the first, an abstraction, as you'll recall, is any thing that's not the thing itself (even a name, or the simplest of descriptions).

Stevens intends this injunction more narrowly, though; he's talking about those temporary agreements between internal and external which serve as the basis for further imaginative work: when "Life's nonsense pierces us with strange relation." These are "not balances / That we achieve but balances that happen" (which shouldn't be taken to mean that the process is passive: "The habit of probing for an integration seems to be part of the general will to order," as he says elsewhere), and that constitute our most profound experiences—"moments of awakening, / Extreme, fortuitous, personal, in which / We more than awaken, sit on the edge of sleep, / As on an elevation." To awaken is to overcome habitual human projections "And see the sun again with an ignorant eye / And see it clearly in the idea of it." For Stevens, abstraction is also the ability to generalize from specifics. This kind of insight is always modest: "The final elegance, not to console / Nor sanctify, but plainly to propound."

Because flux is the only constant both within us and without, the Supreme Fiction must necessarily change (Stevens's second injunction). This is a little tricky because an aesthetic object is a crystallization of experience; that's the great gift of it, that it sort of suspends time. But Stevens's point is not just that appearances or properties are altered over time, it's that the stuff of life itself is change (ideas or concepts, on the other hand, are already ossified): "The casual is not / Enough. The freshness of transformation is // The freshness of a world. It is our own, / It is ourselves, the freshness of ourselves, / And that necessity and that presentation // Are rubbings of a glass in which we peer." This is what Nietzsche was getting at with his notion of constant becoming, an ongoing flux which necessarily implies not only 'freshness' but also inevitable decline—and death. The dialectical work (the "more than casual"), while constant, must not only be open and flexible enough to allow for its own recurring transformation over the long haul, it must be change (and not merely illustrate some systematic theory).

Finally, the Supreme Fiction must give pleasure, which, to me, means it is beautiful—and therefore also means it embodies *significant form*. There's much more to say about the equation implicit in that last sentence, but for now the point is that a sort of wholeness, or even just the suggestion of wholeness, is the ultimate objective of the poem (or the song or the photograph): "there is an hour / Filled with expressible bliss, in which I have // No need, am happy, forget need's golden hand, / Am satisfied without solacing majesty, And if there is an hour there is a day, // There is a month, a year, there is a time / In which majesty is a mirror of the self: / I have not but I am and as I am, I am."

Stevens demands that the fiction 'suffice' (a favorite word of his) and that we accept that all meaning resides in metaphor, but there's an even bigger and more general point to be made about this: the very fact that there are three 'rules' means that he sees a way of managing the form-making process, and clearly from a remove. You can be mired (because you have no other choice) in the moment-to-moment sense-making of everyday life (which inevitably results in fictions) and yet you can also extract yourself from the process, observe the fiction, and shape it to its and your benefit—to make it *useful*. This is "the power over the mind that lies in the mind itself, the incalculable expanse of the imagination as it reflects itself in us and about us."

This is all, primarily, in Stevens's poem, related to the qualities of an aesthetic object. But the knock-out punch is that this approach to poetry can be extrapolated and reframed as a way to live your life: an *ethics* built on an *aesthetic* position (a concept to which we will return): "The final belief is to believe in a fiction, which you know to be a fiction, there being nothing else. The exquisite truth is to know that it is a fiction and that you believe it willingly." To really fully inhabit it: to know (to *internalize*) that the whole thing is fragile and fleeting and fabricated, but to go with the flow nonetheless—but also to own it and actively intervene in the imaginative mechanism, *to behave objectively toward your subjectivity*, and to put yourself "relentlessly in possession of happiness." Because this is really truly attainable, and rest assured: no other force on earth is going to step up and do any of this shit for you.

...

The judgments we make of the quality and usefulness of fictions (this includes scrutiny of our own, as well as those of others) are most sound when grounded in the empirical.

The real is only the base, but it is the base.
—ws

"Although we live in the mind, the source of our satisfactions is in the earth," writes Joseph N. Riddel, who identified the "natural inversion of religious orthodoxy" in Stevens's desire in poetry "to create heavens in the image of earth," *instead of the other way around.*

9   On the other hand: "The subject-matter of poetry is not that 'collection of solid, static objects extended in space' but the life that is lived in the scene that it composes," Stevens writes, and this is crucial because "what reality lacks is a *noeud vital* with life."

45

The liberating embrace of the real is essential to our most valuable and enduring fictions.

Consider this a metaphysics of the actual.

10   When I was a kid, I read *The Hobbit*, like all my friends, and then tried *The Lord of the Rings*, but none of it seemed to take. An adult neighbor who was a voracious reader gave me her Stephen King paperbacks as she finished them, and those held my attention better, especially the few without anything supernatural going on. When I'd exhausted King, let's say I was 13 or 14, she gave me *The World According to Garp*. Which was eye-opening to say the least: I didn't know exactly what adults did and how they treated one another, but it seemed that I could test *Garp* against what I could actually observe daily. So when I read somewhere (after inhaling *Owen Meany* and *Hotel New Hampshire*, etc.) that John Irving was a Jamesian novelist, I was off to the races. I don't think my literary heart has ever beaten faster with trepidation than during the entirely civil conversation between Kate and Merton at the end of *The Wings of the Dove*.

"The incredible is not a part of poetic truth," Stevens writes. "On the contrary, what concerns us in

[Based on what I've said so far, it may seem a surprise to trot out a word like 'metaphysics.' And even more so to relate the term specifically to the real.

"If we consider the nature of our experience when we are in agreement with reality, we find, for one thing, that we cease to be metaphysicians... we do not want to be metaphysicians," says Stevens, and that had been my

poetry, as in everything else, is the belief of credible people in credible things. It follows that poetic truth is the truth of credible things, not so much that it is actually so, as that it must be so. It is toward that alone that it is possible for the intelligence to move."

Throughout, I will argue for the necessity of the credible, for an approach that leans more towards the objective while honoring the subjective. "The balancing of subjective and objective vision assumes enough time to come to conclusions about oneself, the world, and their right relation," writes Robert Adams. Although he notes that when it comes to making things, "as Goethe observed about poets, 'a subjective nature has soon talked out his little internal material, and is at last ruined by mannerism,' whereas a more objective nature 'is inexhaustible, and can always be new,' taking as it does for inspiration and consolation the whole world beyond the private one."

I believe that photographic truth is precisely the truth of the credible.

position for a long time. Indeed, metaphysics seemed to me to encompass evidence-free assertions of absolute certainty, when all I saw was fragmented and conditional, a world not so much irrational as simply non-rational.

Marilynne Robinson changed my attitude toward the word (though not the world) when I came across this in an essay: "So great is my respect for secular people that I wish they had a metaphysics worthy of them. I would be very interested to see a secularism based on contemporary science, though I grant the difficulty of deriving a metaphysics from anything as surpassingly dynamic and complex as the universe has proved to be at every scale, and continuously open to reconception as our understanding of it must be."

My initial thought was that I didn't see anything wrong with science as a metaphysics, and that complexity and change made it all the more appealing. (Actually, my very first reaction was mild shock that Robinson had the capacity to be even faintly condescending to us non-believers; I can find no similar instance in either her fiction or nonfiction.) But mostly I was intrigued by her use of the indefinite article.

It's all about the human urge to synthesize experience—to get at a meaning, if not necessarily the meaning. Each of us has a 'physics' (the sensory input from outside the self) and a 'metaphysics,' which is whatever internal mental glue we use to hold together all the external stuff. Riddel, writing on Stevens: "Out of desire and despair, man aesthetically reconstructs his world, discovering his metaphysical in the physical. What he makes—these many 'sensuous worlds'—are makings of himself."

At root, a metaphysics is a how *for the* what—*an approach to life—and that of course is what it has always been, in any traditionally prescribed set of universal values. But rather than be servant to an established metaphysics, our challenge is to create one (or perhaps several: "There are many truths, / But they are not parts of a truth," Stevens wrote) that serves each of us individually.*

While one's metaphysical outlook will ultimately be personal and particular, it is apt to have characteristics in common with those of like-minded people and groups, all of which can be discussed, debated, and refined. "Art reveals reality and because there is a way in which things are," says Murdoch, "there is a fellowship of artists."

This cultivation is important because a metaphysics should lead to an ethics of behavior, in the way that any theory implies a practice. "The relation of art to life is of the first importance especially in a skeptical age," Stevens writes, "since, in the absence of a belief in God, the mind turns to its own creations and examines them, not alone from the aesthetic point of view, but for what they reveal, for what they validate and invalidate, for the support that they give."

As Nietzsche said, "Only as an aesthetic phenomenon is the world justified eternally."]

A deliberate deference to the real is essential to the second sense of decreation: an intentional scrutiny of the calibration between mind and world, *to the advantage of the latter.* Murdoch called this the act of 'unselfing': a process whereby the not-self is allowed to press back against the self, with the goal (ultimately impossible) of eliminating our projections. (Creation—the opposing process—is in this context the projection of the self's received ideas and ideologies onto the world.)

Alas, no matter how clear-headed and decreative our aspirations toward the actual, we exist in fictions, in abstractions. This is our fate. "We live in the center of a physical poetry, a geography that would be intolerable except for the non-geography that exists there," Stevens wrote. Thus the never-ending need for the Supreme Fiction—not just the everyday fiction that is an automatic function of being human, but a heightened, active, and *useful* fiction.

> We cannot be rid of illusions. Illusion is our natural condition. Why not accept it?
> —JG

Accepting illusions (abstractions) is much easier said than done, however; it must be acknowledged that no matter how much I tell myself or you that it's okay to dwell in fictions, it just doesn't sit quite right. We long for a direct unabstracted connection between self and not-self. Eden has its effect because we know, every moment of every day, how it feels to be cast out.

The ache for completion is unquenchable and never-ending. Despite our immense powers of imagination, the ideal and the real will never line up to our satisfaction, and we will never transcend our limitations; this accounts for all sufferings great and small. We are forever "an unhappy people in a happy world," Stevens says.

> The absurd is born of this confrontation between the human need and the unreasonable silence of the world… the Absurd is not in man… nor in the world, but in their presence together. For the moment it is the only bond uniting them.
> —ALBERT CAMUS (ACa)

Fortunately, we do occasionally catch a glimpse of wholeness, however ephemeral. We experience moments of transcendence when a rich formal relationship is felt as its equivalent: beauty.

We rely heavily on these convergences.

> Every moment some form grows perfect in hand or face; some tone on the hills or the sea is choicer than the rest; some mood of passion or insight or intellectual excitement is irresistibly real and attractive for us—for that moment only.
> —WALTER PATER (WP)

> James Joyce has taught us the word "epiphany," a showing forth—Joyce had the "theory" that suddenly, almost miraculously, by a phrase or a gesture, a life might thrust itself through the veil of things and for an instant show itself forth, startling us by its existence. In itself the conception of the epiphany

*["Why is Form beautiful?" Robert Adams asks.
"Because, I think, it helps us meet our worst fear, the
suspicion that life may be chaos and that therefore our
suffering is without meaning." For me, as I've already
made clear, this is more than a suspicion, it is a certitude: our misery is indeed meaningless. This fear,
though, drives me and Adams to the same place.*

*"Form in a picture is justified by our experience of
wholeness (coherence) in life," he writes elsewhere, "and
if we are to be convincingly reminded by art of such
experience then the shape in art has to be believably
tentative, as fragile as meaning seems to be in life."]* 11

11   The connection of form to the epiphany was so
obvious to Nietzsche that he used the term "ultimate beauties." These, according to Pearson, are

The glimpse is not without its cost. The transience of our epiphanies is a melancholy reminder (painful, but not entirely so) of our actual bodily transience in this world.

But death, being so much more approachable—either here or just around the bend—has always been an influence. What I mean to say is that death is common. If you are having a good time and you conceive the possibility that the good time will end, then you are concerned with death, though in a mild and unremarkable way. But what I want to get to is something else: that death is the central concern of lyric poetry. Lyric poetry reminds us that we live in time. It tells us that we are mortal. It celebrates or recognizes moods, ideas, events only as they exist in passing. For what meaning would

experienced "at singular, rare and precarious moments of life and have no objective existence independent of such moments. They do not disclose to us anything about the world, but are bound up with the desire of our seeing." Nietzsche wrote that life "consists of rare individual moments of the highest significance and countless intervals in which at best the phantoms of those moments hover about us."

We say of an encounter with beauty that it is 'pierc-
ing' or that it 'killed' or 'slayed'—with good reason,
and in a good, healthy way. "That old assassin, heart's
desire," Stevens wrote.

And just as significant form in a poem or picture
evokes the brevity of our lives, the opposite is equally
true: "Death is the mother of beauty."

Stevens is expressing here not the cliché that the
transient things of earth become more precious,
hence more beautiful, as we feel them to be transient,
but the profounder idea that all the beauty we as
human beings can know is born of the process of
change which is one with the process of death.
—MARIE BOROFF (MB)

This is the supreme and abiding irony: our greatest weaknesses—transience of body plus limitation of mind (i.e., our meaninglessness)—are the only reasons that anything (all the products of our imaginative bodies and minds) has any significance at all.

—WS

II

FROM THIS
THE POEM
SPRINGS

Each and every one of us suffers the breach between *what is* and *what is not.* Our selves are merely the sum of our idiosyncratic formal strategies for dealing with this separation of world and mind.

This fundamental disconnect—and our response to that estrangement—is the reason aesthetic objects like poems, paintings, and symphonies exist. (And also philosophy, which Wittgenstein considered akin to poetry: "There is indeed the inexpressible.")

> Every sorrow suggests a thousand songs, and every song recalls a thousand sorrows, and so they are infinite in number, and all the same. 12
>
> —MR

12   Valéry tells us that "There are productions of ideas or acts whose aim is not to modify the things around us but to modify ourselves, to dispel a kind of interior

Curiously, though, not all of us are compelled to make durable things out of what is impermanent. So the question is: why do *any* of us make aesthetic objects?

I've written about the myriad relationships that constitute the self: those engendered when the imagination creates an accord between the internal and the external. These associations comprise not only things (or people, a subset of things) but also time.

discomfort, a sickness that no act relieves directly." Likewise, Rilke's "project was to find, in art, a way to transform the emptiness, the radical deficiency, the human longing into something else," says Robert Hass. So far, my subject has been the permanent brokenness; what it can be turned into will be our next concern.

Earlier I mentioned that the initial recognition of the separation between self and not-self is seen by many as a 'fall from grace.' This implies some generic previous wholeness, but also more specifically speaks to a religious beneficence. I can see no evidence for the former (unless to be whole is to lack consciousness, an even sadder state of affairs), so the latter is

Our experience of the present is profoundly conditioned by our accumulated personal memory. Because this autobiographic past is so utterly idiosyncratic, our unique perceptions—each an intersection of *past and present*—are precisely what individuates us.

To refine: Our selves consist of fluctuating sets of imaginative correlations between time (*what is not*, or the internal past up to this moment) and things (*what is*, the external present at this moment). Each

certainly out of the question. Which is just a restatement of my conviction that all meaning is generated internally.

And yet I'm deeply enthralled by the existentially wounded work of some people who believe that there is indeed a universal meaning of external origin. Of the artists I hold in the very highest regard, there are two in particular (that I know of, because they've made it clear) for whom Christianity is important: Marilynne Robinson and Sufjan Stevens. I bring them up because I know their works thoroughly enough to have a good understanding of the sort of relationship in which they find themselves—through art—vis-à-vis of us is constantly acting upon current facts based on what we know from previous experience, with the aim of influencing future states of events.

In other words: we hope.

The making of aesthetic objects is a specific and unique expression of this hope.

In an essay on the art of literature, Vladimir Nabokov posits the future as a *thing*, not just as a potentiality.

the world. And the one thing I can say with confidence (and with all due respect) is that these two sense acutely the same limitations—of the actual and of time—that I do. This book's epigraph is drawn from a song called "John My Beloved" in which Sufjan asks: "So can we pretend sweetly / Before the mystery ends?" Yes, please: lots of sweet pretending—in poems and songs and pictures—in what little wondrous time we have left.

I couldn't agree more with Robinson when she places us firmly in the actual: "I'm not terribly persuaded by the word supernatural. I don't like the idea of the world as an encapsulated reality with intrusions

He sets this up by describing a moment when past and present collide to create a particularly lush imaginative space:

> A passerby whistles a tune at the exact moment that you notice the reflection of a branch in a puddle which in its turn, and simultaneously, recalls a combination of damp green leaves and excited birds in some old garden, and the old friend, long dead, suddenly steps out of the past, smiling and closing his dripping umbrella.

He then says, "The inspiration of genius adds a third ingredient: it is the past and the present and the future (your book) that come together in a sudden flash..."

made upon it selectively. The reality that we experience is part of the whole fabric of reality. To pretend that the universe is somewhere else doing something is really not true. We're right in the middle of it. Utterly dependent on it, utterly defined by it. If you read somebody like Wallace Stevens, he's basically saying the same thing."

Now, clearly, she is leaving ample room for mystery in there (while also using as backup an atheist poet, whom she has said elsewhere is among her favorites). But still: in Robinson's fiction and in Sufjan's music, the notion that this limited earthly existence is all we have is so pervasive that I cannot

That little parenthetical holds the whole game: for the artist, the briefest correspondence with the real offers more than just temporary resolution; sometimes it produces an excess, a profligacy that reports itself precisely as a (future) *thing* like a book—or a poem, or a photograph.

sense in either any real belief in some benevolent overseer, or in an afterlife.

Perhaps the value that Robinson and Sufjan Stevens find in everyday life and express in their works is their intuition of the divine. It's a concept that I otherwise reject, but I'm intrigued by Robinson's assertion, in the essay called (conveniently enough) "The Divine," that "our experience is a brilliant translation of the infinite and volatile complexities of Being itself into a world and universe that, remarkably or providentially, seem to lie within our grasp."

I am greatly pleased by that 'or.' I find Being remarkable, and she finds it providential. "It is the belief and not the god that counts," Wallace Stevens wrote.

Roy Harvey Pearce says that "Poetic understanding... is a matter of postulation, not inference," and that the self "reveals its meaning to itself in the creative acts it performs out of its rockbound faith in its own ability to make such postulations." It's this looking forward—specifically the feat of making, *the self revealing itself to itself*—rather than any looking back, that makes the poet.

For Stevens, the poem (that "queer assertion of humanity") arises

As if nothingness contained a métier,
A vital assumption, an impermanence
In its permanent cold, an illusion so desired

That the green leaves came and covered the high rock,
That the lilacs came and bloomed, like a blindness
    cleaned,
Exclaiming bright sight, as it was satisfied,
In a birth of sight.

A *métier* is an occupation. The present moment—the rich permutation of stored memory and emergent perception—may not exactly be *nothing*, but it is a *nothingness* (the foundational emptiness between self and not-self), and, for some, that absence begs a material response. It is a task for the maker to complete, an obligation to fulfill with the assertion of a new and lasting thing (some leaves to cover the rock) summoned from a compulsion to hold together past, present, and future.

Nabokov describes the assumption of this calling as the "passage from the dissociative stage to the associative one."

Pearce echoes this: "The task of poetry, thus its form and function, is somehow to transform intimations into convictions, to see the dilemma all the way through to an end triumphant in its very bitterness."

Bitter ends indeed. Because our convictions (as manifested in our aesthetic objects) will not—and cannot—live up to our intimations of wholeness. "I know better than to claim any completeness for my picture," says Emerson. "I am a fragment, and this is a fragment of me."

The underlying conundrum:

> Our selves are a complex mix of formal relationships *between the internal and the external.*

> Our aesthetic objects can only be constructed of formal relationships *between entirely external things.*

The accords that comprise the self cannot be described—not in words, not in pictures, not in poems or songs or string quartets. Never and nohow. They are by nature ineffable; our inability to get directly at them is the root of our frustrations. 13

13   "I am afraid we are not rid of God because we still have faith in grammar," Nietzsche famously said, and you needn't get tripped up on the atheism to see the point about language in the context of religion doing

The truth is you already know what it's like. You already know the difference between the size and speed of everything that flashes through you and the tiny inadequate bit of it all you can ever let anyone know.

That this is what it's like. That it's what makes room for the universe inside you, all the endless inbent fractals of connection and symphonies of different voices, the infinities you can never show another soul. And you think that makes you a fraud, the tiny fraction anyone else ever sees? Of course you're a fraud, of course what people see is never you. And of course you know this, and of course you try to manage what part they see if you know it's only a part. Who wouldn't? It's called free will, Sherlock. But at the same time it's why it feels so good to break down and cry in front of others, or to laugh, or speak in tongues, or chant in Bengali—it's not English anymore, it's not getting squeezed through any hole.

So cry all you want. I won't tell anybody.

—DAVID FOSTER WALLACE (DFW)

too much to ease the pain instead of too little. Because we're wired for subject-verb-direct object thought processes, we view all things or situations as having been caused. Which thus requires a reason—a primary actor that is both cause of and solution to the human conundrum—where never there was one.

John Gray fascinatingly takes it further: "Atheism does not mean rejecting 'belief in God.' It means giving up belief in language as anything

Do you see a pattern here: a parallel between the
limitations of living and those of making?

If each and every human being despairs at the gap
between the internal ideal and the external real, the
artist despairs more deeply at the limits upon what
can actually be *made* of that gap (or even spoken
out loud, for that matter).

The best we can do is to model the internal by making something that brings significant form to bear

other than a practical convenience. The world is not
a creation of language, but something that—like the
God of the negative theologians—escapes language.
Atheism is only a stage on the way to a more far-
reaching skepticism."

on the external—always a compromise between *what is not* and *what is.*

As engineers like to say: all models are wrong, but some are useful. Wrong, in this case, in two very specific ways:

1. The aesthetic object (this goes for language too) always necessarily fails the self. As Herman Melville wrote, "For whatever is truly wondrous and fearful in man, never yet was put into words or books." No medium can extract from you what you so desperately want to get out.

2. The object also betrays the not-self. We simply cannot speak, or sing or draw, truly of the world that we interact with. "Literature is based not on life but on propositions about life, of which this is one," Stevens said. 14

Despite all this failure, the models we make can still be useful. Triumph is possible, but it is hard won, and in order to judge correctly their success we must look very closely and thoughtfully at

14   As Emerson understands, these two complaints are ultimately one and the same, because they are innate to experience. He recognizes "the inequality between every subject and every object," and says that never "can any force of intellect attribute to the object the proper deity which sleeps or wakes forever in every subject. Never can love make consciousness and ascription equal in force. There will be the same gulf between every me and thee as between the original and the picture."

Wittgenstein wrote: "And this is how it is: if only you do not try to utter what is unutterable then *nothing* gets lost. But the unutterable will be—unutterably—*contained* in what has been uttered!"

the limitations and possibilities of the things we make—a discernment ultimately of their benefit to lived lives. Of their ethics.

15   The goal is to not only make peace with the limitations of the aesthetic object, but to exploit and even rejoice in them. Frank Doggett recasts the failure of a text as "the secrecy that must prevail between the poet and his poem;" therein lies its "never-resolved meaning, its possibility." It is certain that no reader will ever fully understand the self that the maker couldn't fit to the made, so the precise impetus to the

The basic thing to understand is that the aesthetic object is only ever 'about' itself; it is not a bullet point supporting a thing or a concept external to it (and not even in these pages, mind you). It is a concentration or a displacement of immediate experience that is strictly true to neither memory nor moment. "Regardless of historic fact," Szarkowski wrote, "a picture is about what it appears to be about."

> I meant *nothing* by The Lighthouse... Whether right or wrong I don't know, but directly I'm told what a thing means, it becomes hateful to me.
> —VIRGINIA WOOLF (VW)

> A poem is tough by no quality it borrows from a logical recital of events nor from the events themselves but solely from the attenuated power which draws perhaps many broken things into a dance by giving them thus a full being.
> —WCW

poem (as well as the kind and degree of the failure) must remain secret. But the aesthetic object is a new thing in the world, to be judged by the possibilities—the meanings—it has brought into being. These meanings are never resolved because 1) they are unique to each individual reader, and 2) as Stevens asserted, they must remain stubbornly potential, changing over time for any particular reader.

As Emerson said, the poem "has an architecture of its own, and adorns nature with a new thing."

It succeeds or fails on that basis alone.

> A sense of itself is what the poem sponsors, and not a sense of the world. It invents itself: its own necessity or urgency, its tone, its mixture of meaning and sound are in the poet's voice. It is in such isolation that it engenders its own authority... It is not knowledge but rather some occasion for belief, some reason for assent, some avowal of being.
> —MARK STRAND (MS)

> Great variety is possible in the process of transmutation of emotion... but the difference between art and the event is always absolute.
> —T.S. ELIOT (TSE)

> It's not a question of painting life, it's a question of bringing painting alive.
> —PIERRE BONNARD (PB)

This is all to say that our judgment of the usefulness of the work must be limited to how that text lives within us.

> A piece of fiction must be very much a self-contained dramatic unit. This means that it must carry its meaning

inside it. It means that any abstractly expressed com-
passion or piety or morality in a piece of fiction is only
a statement added to it. It means that you can't make
an inadequate dramatic action complete by putting a
statement of meaning on the end of it or in the middle
of it or at the beginning of it. 16
—FO'C

The point is that our aesthetic objects—as provisional intimations of completion—disclose no
reliable information about worldly facts. Nor do
they—or *can* they—reveal the biography of the
maker.

Some try to reconstruct the poets' secret designs
and, with deceptive clarity, read intentions and allu-
sions into their works. With a complacency that
shows where they go wrong, they like to study what
is known (or thought to be known) about an author's
life; as though one could ever know its true inner

16   Or on a didactic wall text.

development, and moreover, as though the beauties
of expression and the delightful harmony—always…
providential—of terms and sounds were the more
or less natural results of the charming or pathetic
incidents of an existence.
—PV

Rather, our made things manifest "desire, set deep in the eye / Behind all actual seeing, in the actual scene, / In the street, in a room, on a carpet or a wall" (Stevens again). Which of course doesn't mean that actual events can't be baked in there.

> It's well to remember that the serious fiction writer always writes about the whole world, no matter how limited his particular scene. For him, the bomb that was dropped on Hiroshima affects life on the Oconee River, and there's not anything he can do about it.
> —FO'C

Desire (memory; mind; *what is not*) and scene (sensory input; the world; *what is*) collide to create a new aesthetic relationship that is independent of both. "I draw the veil off things with words," Woolf said. 17

17   Karl Ove Knausgård writes that "A work of art is like a point in a system of three coordinates: the particular place, the particular time, the particular person." I've collapsed these into two: the internal flux (the self

Such collision is unavoidable, decreed by the ache of our incompletion, the "hot narrow imperatives of the self," as David Foster Wallace said. 'Desire' and 'ache' are words that hint at but do not entirely capture the ineffable. They express the inexhaustible will to significant form.

A distillation: Art is meant to mollify a longing for completion. In the aesthetic object, form is possibility (whereas subject matter is the given); it is the primary means of getting at this unutterable desire.

[Now, you might protest that, in art, form and subject matter are inextricable. I have no basic qualm with that, but I would limit the full authority of the statement to

and its unique time), and the external flux (the place and its own time). All good.

Iris Murdoch: "Art… not fantasy art, affords us a pure delight in the independent existence of what is *our considerations as the reader or viewer. Because for those who would make photographs, form and subject matter are distinct in meaningful ways. One can't simply slap a form on the world and hope to make anything of value, but the photographer who leaves the house with one camera, one lens, and one film stock has surely made some crucial formal decisions before setting eyes on anything at all.*

Szarkowski gets at the crux of the issue: "The ambitious photographer, not satisfied by so tautological a success [that the picture's form and subject matter are indistinguishable] seeks those pictures that have a visceral relation to his own self and his own privileged knowledge, those that belong to him by genetic right, in which form matches not only content but intent.

excellent. Both in its genesis and its enjoyment it is a thing totally opposed to selfish obsession. It invigorates our best faculties... It is able to do this partly by virtue of something which it shares with nature: a perfection of form which invites unpossessive contemplation and resists absorption into the selfish dream life of the consciousness." My only objection here is that one shouldn't think of nature as having a perfection of form. The world just is. Form is human overlay. But amen to resisting absorption.

"This suggests that [photographs] are no more interesting than the person who made them, and that their intelligence, wit, knowledge, and style reach no further than that person's—which leads us away from the measurable relationships of art-historical science toward intuition, superstition, blood-knowledge, terror, and delight."

I've left that word 'content' intact here so as not to damage the echo with 'intent,' but remember: I'm using 'content' to mean the totality of the picture, the form and the subject matter together. And do note Szarkowski's thoughts on self and idiosyncratic understanding ("blood-knowledge"—writing like this is why he stands apart still), and particularly the equation of content and intent, because we'll come back to that in the next section.]

Form is thus the essence of art. Just as form-making is the fundamental activity of us meaning-hungry creatures.

This function is critical: "Form leads its audience into assenting to the possibilities which it creates," says Pearce.

The reality of a fiction derives not from life itself
(which is all chaos and confusion) so much as from
the art (or form) of the writer.
—HENRY JAMES (HJ)

Subject matter is the effable, and its direct communication is journalism (a noble profession, but not the one I'm concerned with).

[I've already defined 'form' in the photograph as everything except the physical stuff that was in front of the lens, and I'll consider formal choices in the use of the camera in Part III. For now, Mark Strand is appropriately loose in regards to the general term: "Form, it should be remembered, is a word that has several meanings, some of which are near opposites. Form has to do with the structure or outward appearance of something, but it also has to do with its essence. In discussions of poetry, form is a powerful word for just that reason:

structure and essence seem to come together, as do the disposition of words and their meaning."]

All form is an effect of character.
—RWE

What is "form" for anyone else is "content" for me. 18
—PV

My first proposition is that the style of the poem and the poem itself are one.
—WS

Style and structure are the essence of a book; great ideas are hogwash.
—VLADIMIR NABOKOV (VN)

The swift sensuous intake is essential, since our response, as readers, must always run even with, if not ahead of, understanding. Basically, our knowledge of a poem serves simply to explain why we were shaken. It will never, alone, do the shaking.
—WILLIAM H. GASS (WHG)

18   Keep in mind that form is a fully human construct and is fallible, just as we are. "Conflict… between the will to express and the means of expression [is] the very basis of art," Knausgård says. "Where the divergence is great, form becomes a problem, and we understand that it always is, that it is never natural, always arbitrary."

Which is not at all to say that important intellectual
elements (of a sort) cannot be in the picture or poem.

*["Kant stresses that beauty appeals to a faculty apart
from understanding: he is never more emphatic than
when he maintains that the response to beauty is a feeling, not a thought," Jerry L. Thompson explains. "But
he is equally clear in explaining how the sense of the
beautiful can attach conceptual thought—how ideas
of things can come into play as part of an aesthetic
response—in a process that stimulates, or enlivens, the
understanding as well as the sense of beauty."*

19   Passions run high on this topic. Roger Fry:
"No one who has a real understanding of the art
of painting attaches any importance to what we
call the subject of a picture—what is represented."
Stevens is on the same page: "I am sorry that a
poem of this sort has to contain any ideas at all,
because its sole purpose is to fill the mind with the
images and sounds that it contains. A mind that
examines such a poem for its prose contents gets
absolutely nothing from it." And James: "We are

82

Crucially, Kant himself sets some specific and meaningful constraints on the kind of "ideas of things" he's talking about: "Where an author owes a product to his genius, he does not himself know how the ideas for it have entered his head, nor has he it in his power to invent the like at pleasure, or methodically, and communicate the same to others in such precepts as would put them in a position to produce similar products."

Described this way, conceptual thought remains very much internal, and, obviously, ineffable outside of the aesthetic object; Valéry, who said that "the 'ideas' that figure in a poetic work do not play the same part, are

ridden by the old conventionalities of type and small proprieties of observance—by the foolish baby-formula (to put it sketchily) of the picture and the subject."

Ever diplomatic, Szarkowski acknowledges that makers try to have it both ways: "Artists themselves tend to take absolutist and unhelpful positions when addressing themselves to questions of content, pretending with Degas that the work has nothing to do with ballet dancers, or pretending with James Agee that it has nothing to do with artifice. Both positions have the virtue of neatness, and allow the artist to answer unanswerable questions briefly and then get back to work. If an artist were to admit that he was uncertain as to what part of the content of his work

not at all currency of the same kind, as the ideas in prose" would be untroubled. We're still very much in the realm of form.]

And yet the topical must be tightly reined in: "The highest lyrical works are those in which the subject, with no remaining trace of mere matter, sounds forth in language until language itself acquires a voice," Theodor Adorno wrote, "this is why the lyric reveals itself to be the most deeply grounded

answered to life and what part to art, and was perhaps even uncertain as to precisely where the boundary between them lay, we would probably consider him incompetent."

When discussing some photographs that he admires, Robert Adams notes: "their beauty is not, to repeat, solely a matter of related shapes. Beauty is, at least in part, always tied to subject matter."

Okay, sure, *in part*. But if the given is your primary concern, it's going to be difficult to make anything novel. There's nothing new under the sun, after all. Happily, on the flipside, the possible is inexhaustible: "There may never be anything new to say," Flannery O'Connor writes, "but there is always a new way to say it, and since, in art, the way of saying a thing becomes a part of what is said, every work of art is unique and requires fresh attention."

in society when it does not chime in with society, when it communicates nothing." 20

[Honoré de Balzac's] plan was to handle, primarily, not a world of ideas, animated by figures representing those ideas, but the packed and constituted, the palpable, provable world before him, by the study of which ideas would inevitably find themselves thrown up.
—HJ

Form, the "sounding forth in language," can be thought of as the metaphysics of the aesthetic object. It is *how*—not *what*—the thing means.

20   Amen to the refusal of poetry, or of *any* aesthetic object, to function as a politics or an ideology. And I'm not even sure that it can. "It is difficult / to get the news from poems," Williams famously wrote. (And yet of course "men die miserably every day / for lack / of what is found there".)

It will seem to some that I'm going in the exact wrong direction in wanting to decouple the photograph from specific societal concerns, but I'm all in with Christopher Beha, who makes "a political case for disengagement" by insisting that we "bear in mind the defining feature of totalitarian societies: they are places in which all modes of life are subsumed under the political, in which each citizen's most important relationship must be his or her relationship to the state." For those of us who would withdraw, "the

The long and short of all this is that normally, when we look at a picture or statue, we *think* the subject and *feel* the form, and express the first in rich and varied language intelligible to everyone, while we only indicate the effect of the other on us in vague terms not much more than translations of gestures and cries "I love!" "I'd rather never see it again," etc. The natural process for going into art is either "So this is Apollo"—or else "O Apollo," etc. But it is not, "What the deuce is the value or importance of this statue?" or "How does it answer to such and such a demand or definition."

—VERNON LEE (VL)

ultimate aim of scaling back our political attention is not apathy but the creation of autonomous space for social, spiritual, and aesthetic experiences. If creeping totalitarianism is your worry, such work is not a form of acquiescence but a form of resistance."

Moreover, politically motivated art-making generally enfeebles the principles and does worse to the object. "We are apt to be misled by some convention or other as to the sort of feeler that we ought to put forth... we have doubtless often enough the courage of our opinions (when it befalls that we have opinions)," Henry James wrote, "but we have not so constantly that of our perceptions." When Williams said, "No ideas but in things," what he equally meant was *no ideas in other ideas*. An abstraction based on an already-existing abstraction can easily slip away into nothingness.

It's fruitful to consider in this context David

Wojnarowicz, whose work is often thought of as
'political.' It seems to me that Eliot could have been
referring directly to him: "I should say that the poet
is tormented primarily by the need to write a poem."
Although the source of the anguish is different
(Eliot's as a matter of aesthetic or spiritual posture;
Wojnarowicz's as a result of societal disapproval of
the gender of those whom he desired), 'tormented' is
I think precisely the right word for Wojnarowicz, and
yet he triumphed because he was first and foremost
a person who would make beautiful things out of the
stuff of his life. And that yearning for meaningful form
(which so obviously parallels his romantic longing) is
why he rips your heart out—not the correctness of his
ideology (which, if it pleases you, was there, but which
he deftly made part of his experience and not a topic
for argument). Eliot again: "The material of the artist
is not his beliefs as held, but his beliefs as felt (so far as
his beliefs are part of his material at all)."

The subjugation of beauty to politics might seem
benign, but I think Marilynne Robinson is right in
calling out an attitude that is having a deleterious
effect not only on the things we make, but on *us*: "I
have had students tell me that they had never heard
the word beautiful applied to a piece of prose until

Here we see another parallel: just as a metaphysics (of whatever kind) serves to bring meaning/
wholeness/order to the raw material of immediate
experience for all people, form in the aesthetic object
works to cohere the raw stuff of subject matter.

*['Meaning' and 'wholeness' here are neutral terms. One
may show one's love or one's loathing in a photograph,
and because the subject matter is the same in either, that
showing will be entirely a matter of form.]*

Now obviously there must be a mechanism that
gets us from normal everyday form-making to the

they came to us at the workshop. Literature had been
made a kind of data to illustrate, supposedly, some
graceless theory that stood apart from it... I think this
phenomenon is an effect of the utilitarian hostility to
the humanities and to art, an attempt to repackage
them, to give them some appearance of respectabil-
ity. And yet the beautiful persists, and so do eloquence
and depth of thought, and they belong to all of us because they are the most pregnant evidence we can
have of what is possible in us."

That last sentence is everything; our responsi-
bilities to each other—if they're to mean much at
all—must encompass a commitment to the persistence
of the beautiful. As Beha observes: "People seem to

achieved form of the made object. I mentioned before how past and present collide in a special way for the maker, so that the collision makes itself known as a lasting thing meant to defy transience.

I now want to be much more specific about that process, to consider a sort of metaphysics *of the maker*, which also might—once internalized and disciplined—become a metaphysics *for the maker*. An approach to making. This will be a metaphysics of decreation, in both of its aspects.

Here, in the context of aesthetic objects in general, the focus is on forgetting. In Part III (specific to photographs) our consideration will switch to the decreative relationship between subject and object.

A parallel emerges here, as we will see that forgetting works across the artist's past, present, and future in distinct but related ways, whether the maker realizes it or not.

And happily, once realized, decreative forgetting—as a shaping force—may be actively put to use by the artist.

Before we jump in, let's admit that any for-argument's-sake distinctions between past and present, and particularly between present and future, are fuzzy. Clearly that's the case as a philosophical or scientific question, but I just mean that ultimately the aesthetic object will seamlessly fuse the faculty of idiosyncratic perception of the moment (past + present) with the object-based and object-limited shaping of that perception (present bleeding into future).

THE PAST

Obviously, it's in the context of the past that the word 'forgetting' has its everyday currency. Each of us has forgotten almost every last bit of our direct experience; so little of what we've done and seen and read and heard remains available to us.

Most often this is thought of negatively: as an inconvenience or a failing, as laziness or a sign of diminishing capabilities. And it can be all of those things, for sure.

But forgetting also has a distinctly positive effect: the involuntary erasure of specifics is what shapes us, over time, as specific individuals. 21

21   "The secret of learning is the systematic elimination of excess. We grow, mostly, by dying," says a colleague to Siddhartha Mukherjee in his *New Yorker* piece on neurological disease and genetics.

Better yet: the continuous unwilled winnowing of experience is the reason we have art—or imagination—in the first place, as Wright Morris asserts:

> If we remembered both vibrantly and accurately—a documentary image rather than an impression—the imaginative faculty would be blocked, lacking the stimulus necessary to fill in what is empty or create what is missing. The faculty of artful lying is image making, and not always confined to fiction writers. Precisely where memory is frail and emotion is strong, imagination takes fire.

While the vast majority of our forgetting is passive, a vital subset of it is active; when we purposefully

> In utero and through our teens and twenties, "synapses between nerve cells are generated in great excess, to be pruned back during later development. The elimination of synaptic connections, which results in the constant refinement of neural circuits, like the soldering and resoldering of wires on a circuit board [is a normal occurrence]... Throughout the brain—particularly in the parts involved in cognition, memory, and learning—synapse pruning continues into our first three decades, which suggests that it may be responsible, in part, for the starburst of adaptive learning that characterizes the first decades of human life. We are hardwired not to be hardwired, and this anatomical plasticity may be the key to the plasticity of our minds."

decide what to remember, we are involved in cultivation of the self. We judge and rejudge life's inputs, keeping some and discarding others, all with the goal of having a ready set of useful standards.

The aesthetics of active forgetting necessarily implies an ethics.

> But choose with care. You are what you love. No?
> —DFW

> There are then two ways for memory to destroy imagination: by retaining too many abstractions (thus failing to perceive fresh detail) and by retaining too many details (thus failing to perceive abstractions). The point is worth repeating because two beneficial categories of forgetting recur throughout these notebooks: in one, a mind has become too attached to its concepts or thought-habits and needs to drop them so as to attend again to detail; in the other, a surfeit of detail clogs the flow of thought and must be winnowed so as to see the larger shapes of concept and abstraction.
>
> Let us reclaim forgetting as a component of truth... Let us say that the self is reborn with every breath we take, that it is constantly dropping away and coming into being as conditions alter.
> —LEWIS HYDE (LH)

A judiciously tended set of values supports the sort of open, flexible, and non-literal approach essential to the artist, as Flannery O'Connor says:

> The kind of vision the fiction writer needs to have, or to develop, in order to increase the meaning of his story is called anagogical vision, and that is the kind of vision that is able to see different levels of reality in one image or one situation. [Anagogical vision was] a way of reading nature which included most possibilities... It seems to be a paradox that *the larger and more complex the personal view*, the easier it is to compress it into fiction. (emphasis mine)

Certainly, the richer and more voluminous the self that is shaped from the past, the more that is brought to the present. "Bees ransack flowers here and flowers there," Montaigne wrote, "but then they make their own honey, which is entirely theirs and no longer thyme or marjoram." So ransack away. 22

22   Legend has it that—as a nod to Robert Capa's famous assertion that "If your pictures aren't good, you're not close enough"—Tod Papageorge said, "If your pictures aren't good, you're not reading enough." It sounds like him, but whoever the author is, this gets at the spirit of the thing by placing the locus of achieved meaning in the persistently

THE PRESENT

The actual is constantly demanding of the mind
that it use its powers to manage the chaos of all
that is external to it. This is true foremost of one's
simple (and yet immensely complex) embodied
navigation of the world; the vast majority of what
'happens' in cognition never makes it into consciousness, never becomes part of the narration
that constitutes self. But bits and pieces *do* somehow slip into language.

A sight, an emotion, creates this wave in the mind,
long before it makes words to fit it; and in writing
(such is my present belief) one has to recapture this,

cultivated mind of the maker of the aesthetic object
and, contra Capa, not in the subject matter (or prox-
imity thereto).

and set this working (which has nothing apparently
to do with words) and then, as it breaks and tumbles
in the mind, it makes words to fit it.
—vw

This pressure of the real upon consciousness is especially acute for the maker of aesthetic objects. As Vendler says, "The will to utterance and to constructive form is always solicited anew by the enigmatic appearances of the world; they create horizons for us at the end of the mind, on the edge of space."

For one with the compulsion to utter, the possibilities for the imagination in the present moment are like new horizons, practically limitless. There's work to be done, and some of it quickly; one must complement passively decaying memory with an active decreative forgetting, a deliberate in-the-moment winnowing of the inconsequential, in order to apprehend and influence the shape of what is to be made.

Of course, the type of thing to be made has enormous impact on how much shaping happens in the moment, and how much occurs in the future, and how (or even if) one thinks of the link between the two. 23

However much the work comes into being at the moment of rapture, there remains much to be done later, in recapture. I take these rhyming terms from Nabokov's paraphrases of Russian words for two types of inspiration: *vostorg* and *vdokhnovenie.*

> The pure flame of *vostorg*, initial rapture, has no conscious purpose in view but is all-important in linking the breaking up of the old world with the building up of the new one. When the time is ripe and the writer settles down to the actual composing of his book, he will rely on the second serene and steady

23   The book contemplated by Nabokov is clearly a future creation, perhaps requiring years of work, whereas a few frames of film may be exposed in less than an inspired second. A nascent negative is not yet a photograph, but eventual printing and presentation have been meaningfully limited by choices made at the moment of exposure.

   Similarly, a drawing might be executed—as a sketch for a painting or a complete thing in itself—in just a few minutes. Or a poem written. A melody might be hummed into a recorder for later expansion, a guitar picked up immediately, or notes made for the structure of a symphony.

kind of inspiration, *vdokhnovenie,* the trusted mate
who helps to recapture and reconstruct the world.

And so, we too move from the hot and brief to the
serene and steady...

THE FUTURE

As I said, the boundaries we set between present and
future are slippery. And yet, at some point, according
to Nabokov, there is a perceptible transition when...

> ...fiery *vostorg* has accomplished his task and cool
> *vdokhnovenie* puts on her glasses. The pages are still
> blank, but there is a miraculous feeling of the words
> all being there, written in invisible ink and clamoring
> to become visible.

T.S. Eliot would second that crucial distinction
drawn at the time one puts pen to paper:

> The more perfect the artist, the more completely sep-
> arate in him will be the man who suffers and the mind
> which creates; the more perfectly will the mind digest
> and transmute the passions which are its material.

So, without needing to solve the nature of time, we

can think about the concrete work of shaping, and how it differs from the intangible impulse to make. While also keeping in mind how tightly the later crafting resembles and correlates to the initial stimulus: the former as an embodiment of the latter.

Marilynne Robinson:

> When I write fiction, I suppose my attempt is to simulate the integrative work of a mind perceiving and reflecting, drawing upon culture, memory, conscience, belief or assumption, circumstance, fear, and desire—a mind shaping the moment of experience and response and then reshaping them both as narrative, holding one thought against another for the effect of affinity or contrast, evaluating and rationalizing, feeling compassion, taking offense. These things do happen simultaneously, after all.

> You cannot take heaven by magic.
> —TSE

I like to think of shaping as another, and much more active, form of forgetting. Because we are bringing our imaginative faculty to bear as much on what the object *is not,* as on what it *is.* We are again, as always, in the realm of limitations; but now the maker is (somewhat) in control.

Here, the word 'faculty' should be taken quite seriously, as it is an active marshalling of forces that is required for the object to finally come about. Vigorous shaping shows respect for both one's imagination and one's self. Valéry says, "Clear, distinct operations of the mind are... essential to the dignity of the muse."

It's worth noting that many great artists have been adamant on this point. Arthur Rimbaud famously called poetry a "derangement of the senses," but the adjective right before that was "systematic" (depending on your translation). Flannery O'Connor wrote that fiction must be both canny and uncanny, so that it can properly address the connection between reality and mystery.

Most achingly, Emily Dickinson taught us that the poem can only be attained by an uncomfortable process of extraction.

> Essential Oils—are wrung—
> The Attar from the Rose
> Be not expressed by Suns—alone—
> It is the gift of Screws—

Whether seen as distillation or compression, this

is vital decreative forgetting at work, and the shaping that occurs will be the sole determinant of the usefulness of the eventual object. "For it is not the 'greatness,' the intensity, of the emotions, the components, but the intensity of the artistic process, the pressure, so to speak, under which the fusion takes place, that counts," Eliot writes.

Be aware that this pressure is not exclusively a restrictive force. Alteration is possible, and even desirable, if in service of the real. O'Connor spoke on this:

> St. Thomas called art "reason in making." This is a very cold and very beautiful definition, and if it is unpopular today, this is because reason has lost its ground among us... The artist uses his reason to discover an answering reason in everything he sees. For him, to be reasonable is to find, in the object, in the situation, in the sequence, the spirit which makes itself.
>
> If we admit, as we must, that appearance is not the same thing as reality, then we must give the artist the liberty to make certain rearrangements of nature if these will lead to greater depths of vision. The artist himself always has to remember that what he is rearranging is nature, and that he has to know it and

be able to describe it accurately in order to have the
authority to rearrange it at all... This is not the kind
of distortion that destroys; it is the kind that reveals,
or should reveal. 24

All along, I could have said that the maker—in the
act of shaping—is bringing significant form to bear
on the made. The parallel, as Robinson was getting
at, is that the artist forms her work in the very same
way that anyone (artist or not) forms any moment
of experience, only in a heightened or dislocated
fashion, and with the goal of an object in mind. 25

24   Regarding rearrangement, O'Connor is correct
with respect to writing (and also painting and sculpture). However, as I will argue later, intervention of
this sort, when working with a camera, can undermine or even destroy the type of meaning that is
uniquely *photographic*.

25   Dickinson addressed this heightening or disloca-
tion when she instructed us to:

> Tell all the truth but tell it slant—
> Success in Circuit lies
> Too bright for our infirm Delight
> The Truth's superb surprise
> As Lightning to the Children eased

Just as form organizes the multiple and messy relationships that constitute any human self, form manages the work of art. Or, to be exact: form *is* the self; form *is* the aesthetic object. Which means that none of this is or should be easy, or tidy. "You don't dream up a form and put the truth in it. The truth creates its own form. Form is necessity in the work of art... You are not supposed to feel at home or at ease in any of the forms you see around you. Create your own form out of what you've got, let it take care of itself," according to O'Connor.

The whole game is in the slant: in the conviction that the aesthetic object is not the thing itself (and, as a telling—as an abstraction—couldn't be anyway) but rather a skewed aspect of the thing. Because she trusts us, Dickinson doesn't say exactly how far off plumb she's thinking, and that's where things get interesting. As I mentioned earlier, it's one of the most thrilling experiences of mind to parse out the degrees of fiction in our fictions.

A couple things to note. One: we're called upon to tell *all* the truth, which doesn't mean that we must say everything about the exorbitant factual world of experience (another impossibility), but rather everything

She also wrote: "You are always bounded by what you can make live." In the same spirit, Robinson says that, for the maker of aesthetic objects, "Beauty disciplines." Both remarks are another way of saying "Form disciplines." Robinson here is specifically considering the creation of a fictional character, and finding its proper formal limitations, but the lesson is broadly applicable:

> Practically speaking, when I am writing I tend to think of a character as having a palette or a music. An aesthetic, in other words. While this is in some ways constraining, it establishes the limits within which substantive invention is possible and more to the point, within which variation is meaningful. These

about the idiosyncratic experience itself—the fleeting intersection of self and not-self—all the joy and all the ache.

Two: we are infirm creatures, broken because our inexhaustible desire is profoundly restrained by the actual. So we must take heed: the basic ontological truth of the actual, if somehow we could access it, would be too dazzling for us. Here Robert Adams is instructive: "The Form toward which art points is of an incontrovertible brilliance, but it is also far too intense to examine directly. We are compelled to understand Form by its fragmentary reflection in the daily objects around us; art will never fully define light."

limits liberate the character, a fact that would be accounted a paradox if it were not so familiar.

As a fiction develops, a writer has the exhilarating experience of losing options... After one or two brilliant details, every subsequent choice is disciplined by them... Grace and beauty are, in the same way and in the very fact, intrusions upon authorial intent because the fiction has found its way to its wholeness and completion.

The mind is always in process, moving in time through the currents of possibility, realizing formally meaningful things in and from the flux of consciousness, paragraphs and poems that have an overplus of meaning even the writer would not have recognized if certain words had not come together in a certain order. The ways in which they are satisfying—to the ear, to the senses, to cultural memory—fill them with meaning. So, beauty disciplines. It recommends a best word in a best place and makes the difference palpable between aesthetic right and wrong. And it does this freely, within the limits it finds—cultural, material, generic. Another paradox, perhaps, a discipline that is itself free, and free to make variations on such limits as it does choose to embrace. Beauty is like language in this. It can push at the borders of intelligibility and create new eloquence as it does so. 26

26   Just above, I quickly took the liberty of equating beauty with form; that could use a little explanation. The two have been, to my thinking, essentially the same thing since I read this from Adams: "If the proper goal of art is, as I now believe, Beauty, the

This is why O'Connor and Eliot and all the others are so enthusiastic about a decreative process that could at first be seen as limiting. As we shape, restrict, edit—as we limn and forget—we paradoxically open up unanticipated possibilities and cogencies in the work. From the imposition of form: an unbidden "overplus of meaning."

What's more: in a feedback loop, the made changes the maker. Adam Gopnik says that "words shape ideas and ideas shape souls."

Beauty that concerns me is that of Form."
    When you get down to it, this statement goes further by collapsing art, beauty, and form into aspects of the same thing. Adams would not endorse my equivalence, however, because in his view "Beauty is... a synonym for *the coherence and structure underlying life*." As is clear by now, I don't think there is any preëxisting universal organization (capital-F Form) that we're somehow not noticing; any and all coherence is generated by the minds of human beings. Szarkowski knows it's all in the revery and not the reality: "beauty: that formal integrity which pays homage to *the dream of meaningful life*." (emphasis mine in both quotations).
    I like Robinson's art-making practicality in this regard: "Besides the great interest this phenomenon has always had in itself, beauty is a strategy of emphasis. If it is not recognized, the text is not understood."

Something else happens too: If the work is to succeed, it necessarily becomes impersonal in its making. This is perhaps the most challenging demand of decreative forgetting in the crafting of things, for now what's to be forgotten is *your self*.

A poet's function—do not be startled by this remark—
is not to experience the poetic state: that is a private
affair. His function is to create it in others.
—pv

Simple: if a text is not properly comprehended—a failure of form—then the work fails.

Which is all to say that beauty is a human-made thing, or perhaps even something more like a process or a method; it is manifest in (and not the result of) our perpetual form-making (i.e., anti-chaos) activities. Henry James said that "Beauty comes with expression, expression is creation, it makes the reality, and only in the degree in which it is, exquisitely, expression." The third commandment in "Notes Toward a Supreme Fiction" is that "It Must Give Pleasure." I take Stevens to mean that the poem or the picture must, in a form-less world, achieve beauty in order not only to reign, but even to suffice.

May I be skinned alive before I ever turn my private
feelings to literary account… It's one of my principles
that one must never write down one's self. The artist must be present in his work like God in Creation,
invisible and almighty, everywhere felt but nowhere
seen.

—GUSTAVE FLAUBERT (GF)

His constant refrain in his letters is the impersonality,
as he calls it, of the artist, whose work should consist
exclusively of his subject and his style, without an emotion, an idiosyncrasy *that is not utterly transmuted*…
Such was the part he allotted to form, to that rounded
detachment which enables the perfect work *to live by
its own life*, that he regarded as indecent and dishon-
ourable the production of any impression that was not
intensely calculated. "Feelings" were necessarily crude
because they were inevitably unselected, and selection
(for the picture's sake) was Flaubert's highest morality.
(emphasis mine) 27

—HJ

27   When we learn to be disinterested about
aesthetic objects—especially the products of our
own hearts and minds—we give them a life of their
own, which is really the only life they could ever have
anyway. And perhaps as we come to recognize the
intrinsic value of these things, we can come to see
ourselves and others that way as well: as inherently
autonomous and free. (More on this to come.)

I don't mean that the personal is irrelevant *to the process* (everything I've said up to now should lead one to the conclusion that any worthwhile aesthetic object emanates from the multitudinous self, regardless of its subject matter), but I do mean that any personal relationship to subject matter is irrelevant *to the product*.

One could also say: *poesis* is personal; the poem is impersonal. 28

28   If the word 'impersonal' makes you uncomfortable, maybe 'suprapersonal' will be more to your liking. It's Milan Kundera's adjective for the kind of wisdom shown by Leo Tolstoy in the creation of Anna Karenina, a character who was unsympathetic and deserving of her fate in the first draft of the novel bearing her name. That portrayal changed somewhat, as we know.

"I do not believe that Tolstoy had revised his moral ideas in the meantime," Kundera writes, "I would say rather, that in the course of writing, he was listening to another voice than that of his personal moral conviction. He was listening to what I would call the wisdom of the novel. Every true novelist listens for that suprapersonal wisdom, which explains why great novels are always a little more intelligent than their authors."

The work as more expansive than the maker:

The point of view which I am struggling to attack
is perhaps related to the metaphysical theory of the
substantial unity of the soul: for my meaning is,
that the poet has, not a "personality" to express, but
a particular medium, which is only a medium and
not a personality, in which impressions and experiences combine in peculiar and unexpected ways.
Impressions and experiences which are important for
the man may take no place in the poetry, and those
which become important in the poetry may play quite
a negligible part in the man, the personality.

Poetry is not a turning loose of emotion, but an
escape from emotion; it is not the expression of personality, but an escape from personality. But, of course,
only those who have personality and emotions know
what it means to want to escape from these things.
—TSE

this is another way of getting at Robinson's "surplus of
meaning." Kundera's "wisdom of the novel" is precisely
the "intrusion upon authorial intent" that she ascribes
to beauty, to form. Recall that the aesthetic object
necessarily fails the mind of the maker—Kundera
puts a glorious spin on this: "Not only is the novelist
nobody's spokesperson, but I would go so far as to say
he is not even the spokesperson for his own ideas."
Our unexpected but welcome conclusion: the failure
to be one's own personal representative in one's work
opens up the possibility of the made thing to exceed
the mind of its author, and thus to excel and endure.

I got this Kundera insight from George Saunders,
who closes a crucial practical loop when he observes

The impersonal remove is not even really a matter of choice; it is a basic necessity. As Vendler writes, "A poem, no matter how personal its origin, always requires a selection from, and a linguistic attitude toward, that personal source."

Replace 'linguistic' with 'painterly' or 'musical' or 'photographic' as you wish. Emotions must find strategies in words or pigment or melody; internal relationships cannot be expressed directly but must be made manifest in relationships between external things.

Crucial: Vendler identifies an *attitude* in the text, an idiosyncratic posture or bearing. This is the "emotion which has its life in the poem and not in the history of the poet," as Eliot wrote. All of which is just another way of getting at the idea of *significant form*.

To sum up: one must weed out the personal with respect to subject matter (which is the biographical and the boring) so that the clarifying personality of the aesthetic object (the idiosyncratic and the endlessly thrilling) can bloom. 29

29   And yet, the unique nature of photographic representation ensures that the 'personal' will never cease to be a source of conversation, if not also confusion. Wright Morris got me started on this whole topic many years ago with a statement I found simultaneously shocking and liberating: "Atget is impersonal." The sentence before it is: "We sense that it lies within the province of photography to make both a personal and an impersonal statement."

Now, you might be able to guess which sort of statement it is that Morris prefers, based on his name-drop: "As much as we crave the personal, and insist upon it, it is the impersonal that moves us," he writes. 'Crave' is exactly the right word; that's why we have such a hard time coming to rights with the role of impersonality in aesthetic realization. And yet, it is certainly this detachment which enables the very life of the picture.

Regarding this aspect of the photographic,
Szarkowski provided near-endless food for thought
in the *Mirrors and Windows* exhibition and catalogue.
It will surprise no one that I'm a windows guy (the
more mirrorful pictures lacking much friction from the
actual), though I do admire some mirror-type pictures.
Or rather, I find some of the curator's mirror choices
to actually be windows (and vice-versa). No matter,
though: Szarkowski didn't intend to draw a line in the
sand, and I mention this all just for the insight that follows, and perhaps also to spark interest in a book that
I have found invaluable in thinking about meaning in
photographs:

"The pictures in the first half of this book [mir-
rors] suggest a definition of the word ['personal'] that
leans toward autobiography, or autoanalysis; those of
the second half [windows] reveal concerns that are
personal in the sense that they are not popular. These
concerns may be unfamiliar, eccentric, esoteric, artisti-
cally arcane, stubbornly subtle, or refined to the point

Addressing directly the impersonal in photography, Morris says, "It is the camera that glimpses life as the Creator might have seen it," which is really lovely in its blank-slate, decreative implications—and then he seems to pull his punch: "We turn away as we do from life itself to relieve our sense of inadequacy, of impotence. To those images made in our own likeness, we turn with relief."

Valéry too used the word 'impotence' for the feeling when one is subjected to the starkness of *what is,* and yet I find myself unfamiliar with Morris's reaction to the impersonal photograph (a conduit for *what is* like none other), because even the briefest confrontation with that ache is exactly why I don't turn away but am instead drawn to certain of these pictures without apparently much ability

of aridity, and for any of these reasons we might call them personal. Nevertheless, these pictures might also be called disinterested or objective, in the sense that they describe issues that one might attempt to define without reference to the photographer's presence. Such pictures explore the ways in which photography can translate the exterior world into pictures, which is essentially not a personal but a formal issue."

to resist. (And what's more I find little comfort in the 'personal.')

The goal of the approach that I propose—a metaphysics of decreation for the photographer—is to face (and not to turn away from) the limitations of the camera *and* of life itself (which are very nearly one and the same, as I'll explain) with dignity and assurance, employing an active strategy to meet the incompletion that is our basic human condition—to strike a bargain between *what is* and *what is not*. And then to make something durable from that.

> You've got to discipline yourself to talk out of the part of you that loves the thing, *loves what you're working on.* Maybe just plain loves... I'm not saying I'm able to work consistently out of the premise, but it seems like the big distinction between good art and soso art lies somewhere in the art's heart's purpose, the agenda of the consciousness behind the text. It's got something to do with love. *With having the discipline to talk out of the part of yourself that [can love] instead of the part that just wants to be loved.* I know this doesn't sound hip at all. (emphasis mine)
> —DFW

III

WHICH
ECHOES
BELONG

When I got heavily into Wallace Stevens a few years ago, a lot of nascent ideas began to come together. Oddly enough, I started to think of a *poet* as the patron saint of the kind of photography that I love.

To my reading, his primary concern was to directly engage the limitations common to all of us, and then to live actively and make things fruitfully within those constraints. Over a long career, he seemed always to be scrutinizing the self and the not-self and gauging the gap between the two, and then making the contingent best (a poem) of where he found himself on any given day, at any given moment.

Stevens would surely have endorsed Robert Frank's assertion that it "is always the instantaneous reaction to oneself that produces a photograph." This, in my experience, was what photography was all about: *what is not* meeting *what is* to make not just something new, but something useful. 30

30   Jerry L. Thompson says that the photograph offers "a convincing sense of the physical presence (if not a whole view) of the thing photographed, and also the artist's experience of the picture occasion," which properly places the picture as a thing separate from (though still constituted of) maker and world—an instance unto itself—and links directly to Stevens, whose last line in this section from "An Ordinary Evening in New Haven" could without damage be altered to read: "Photographs of the world are the life of the world."

> The poem is the cry of its occasion,
> Part of the res itself and not about it.
> The poet speaks the poem as it is,
>
> Not as it was: part of the reverberation
> Of a windy night as it is, when the marble
>   statues
> Are like newspapers blown by the wind. He
>   speaks

Actually, with any artform that's much of what's going on. But the thing about making photographs, compared with any other medium, is that our work is way more obviously (and meaningfully) limited by the physicality of the world—and not just by the

> By sight and insight as they are. There is no
> Tomorrow for him. The wind will have passed by,
> The statues will have gone back to be things
>   about.
>
> The mobile and immobile flickering
> In the area between is and was are leaves,
> Leaves burnished in autumnal burnished trees
>
> And leaves in whirlings in the gutters, whirlings
> Around and away, resembling the presence of
>   thought
> Resembling the presences of thoughts, as if,
>
> In the end, in the whole psychology, the self,
> The town, the weather, in a casual litter,
> Together, said words of the world are the life of
>   the world.

For the photographer, there is always no tomorrow. The picture, like the poem, must be made now, else the wind and the clouds and the light—and, what's more, the mood—will have passed on.

actual stuff in front of the camera, but also by the impassivity of time.

But limitations can also be possibilities. In fact, ours directly indicate the fundamental power of the medium: because the constraints of photography align so intimately with those that we all experience every moment, the photograph is absolutely unique in its ability to convey the human conundrum. Working with a camera allows the maker to approach the predicament—and to tentatively resolve it—in ways unmatched by the use of any other tool, and *not just in degree but in kind.*

Assuming that most of us were inspired to start using a camera because of what we'd seen and felt in photographs, I'll start with the object and its distinctive qualities before turning to the maker.

LOOKING AT
PHOTOGRAPHS

Again, the photograph is clearly distinguished from any other aesthetic object by two primary attributes.

> Photographs are profoundly tied to, and limited by, the actual.

> We comprehend photographs as having been made in a vanishingly small amount of time.

To reiterate: the most telling parallel of all is between the constraints of the camera (time and the actual) and those of ordinary human meaning-making (in which the mind constantly manages its ephemeral relationships with real, recalcitrant things). Stevens could have been speaking of the photograph when he wrote:

> These are hymns appropriate to
> The complexities of the world, when apprehended,
>
> The intricacies of appearance, when perceived.
> They become our gradual possession.

As the product of this curious alignment between machine and mind, the photograph is capable of manifesting the transient and the provisional—and thus of becoming a singularly moving work of art. 31

31   Some delimiting: I mentioned earlier how Aristotle approved of the fiction (as opposed to Plato's denunciation of the falsehood) of the aesthetic object. Which is all to the good, but here's the thing: Aristotle is well known in this respect for the idea of catharsis in art (and specifically in tragedy), wherein the fiction establishes the emotional distance for the viewer to pleasurably experience sensations too painful to encounter first-hand. I have no problem with this at all, but it's not what I'm talking about with regard to photographs. It's conceivable that viewing a photograph could be cathartic, but the unique power of the photograph lies in its tight relation to the very moment of experience, a time before joy and pain (and a whole bunch of other stuff) have even been articulated, let alone sorted out. It's just that basic.

Szarkowski makes a related point when he contrasts photographs that rely on the established public meanings of what's depicted with those from which privately generated meanings spring afresh.

"Most photographers deal with meanings that seem intrinsic to their subject matter, or that are at least firmly attached to it by association or tradition. Many meanings are attached to mountains, for example, having to do not only with geography but with innocence, aspiration, retreat, gods and prophets, independence, and loneliness. Most pictures of mountains touch on such generic and inherited meanings, but if they are good pictures they also have a specific and unique meaning, which has to do with the particular experience of an individual artist at a particular place and time.

"Other pictures do not concern themselves with known meanings, but begin with the substance of specific experience: existential fact. Those who make such pictures may hope that generic meanings will accrue to them in time, but this is not a prior condition for making them. The pictures are made to clarify an experience that was for unknown reasons compelling in itself. If this is managed successfully, and if others view the picture and say to themselves, Yes, it is true, then a meaning will probably be discovered in it, or attributed to it."

Robert Adams gets down to practicalities: "One does not for long wrestle a view camera in the wind and heat and cold just to illustrate a philosophy... It is only your enjoyment of a commitment to what you see, *not what you rationally understand*, that balances the otherwise absurd investment of labor." (emphasis mine)

This is probably the most urgent thing I have to say: *We sense in the photograph the very contingency of being alive.* This peculiar kind of picture presents itself as an absolute enigma, just as existence does. 32

Unsurprisingly, the medium's distinguishing features can also be drawbacks; it is due to these characteristics—regarding the actual and the temporal—that photographs are often devalued as aesthetic objects by some, and misunderstood even by those who do

Does all of this remind you of the broader existential suggestion I made earlier? In the absence of any universal external reason for being here, meaning must be wholly internally generated from moment-by-moment experience. This corresponding activity in and of the photograph is not a coincidence.

32   "With Atget we feel no application of artistic principle or sensibility," Szarkowski writes, "only the attempt to describe clearly and precisely what is in front of the camera, but what is out there now seems not secure and objective but contingent, provisional, relative, capable of continual speciation."

I'd take that even further to say that Atget *saw the flux objectively,* that he understood the relativity to be the reality. He knew that nothing was ultimately secure, and he found the appropriate medium for manifesting that unsettled and unsettling knowledge.

appreciate them. So let's work through the ups and downs of all that.

1. THE REAL

The factuality of the photograph is certainly its most defining feature. Nobody 'believes' a painting or a poem in the same way. "However much they may lie," says Wright Morris "[photographs] do so with the raw materials of truth."

The photographer's lies are—on the surface level (an exceedingly important level)—the least fictitious of any maker's. Photographs are even better than poems in proving Stevens's assertion that "There is, in fact, a world of poetry indistinguishable from the world in which we live."

> ...photography is by its nature forced toward doing the old job of art—of discovering and revealing meaning from within the confusing detail of life... Photographs [have] to be built from life directly. Photography is new, I submit, because it is among the few arts that have, through the twentieth century, remained attentive to the facts of this world, to the actual appearance of the place that troubles us. In painting and sculpture it has been lethally easy to

escape right off into some alleged spiritual essence, or
to lounge flabbily around as ornament.

—RA

As a threshold matter, the photograph is persuasive
because it is constructed of the same stuff as everyday experience.

We are convinced by the photograph because we

33   Stieglitz said that "Beauty is the universal seen,"
and right there is the basic problem with much of his
enterprise.

comprehend in it the same predicament we face every day—the friction of the actual that frustrates us at every turn.

> Atget's pictures are thus recognized as a supreme ex-
> pression of most photographers' instinctive faith—
> a belief in the significance of specific scenes, a signif-
> icance fittingly matched to the unique power of the
> camera for precise transcription—and a hesitancy to
> theorize, a disinclination encouraged by the resistance
> offered from such fully recorded specificity.
> —RA

A problem arises, however, when the convincing goes a bit too far and the photograph is mistaken for what is depicted in it.

[Clement Greenberg states the issue plainly, and he's incorrect exactly as someone primarily concerned with painting would be: "The art in photography is literary art before it is anything else: its triumphs and monuments are historical, anecdotal, reportorial, observational before they are purely pictorial." He then identifies as a drawback what I consider an unqualified and unmatched strength: "Because of the transparency of the medium, the difference between the extra-artistic, real-life meaning of things and their artistic meaning is even narrower in photography than it is in prose."

Which leads him to the conclusion that "This is why there are so many pictures made with documentary intent among the masterpieces of photography."

Greenberg does later recognize that the successful photograph requires much more than the topical interest of the subject matter: "But they have become masterpieces by transcending the documentary and conveying something that affects one more than mere knowledge could. The purely descriptive or informative is almost as great a threat to the art in photography as the purely formal or abstract. The photograph has to tell a story if it is to work as art." All good until that last sentence, which overreaches; there's no need for any picture, let alone a photograph, to "tell a story," but I think we can feel comfortable with what he's getting at.

Since Greenberg invoked the literary, perhaps this distinction will help: On the topic of confessional/autobiographical poetry, Dan Chiasson writes: "The phrase 'what happened' is one of the few that still indicates a place outside of rhetoric and trope, in an intellectual culture that has consigned virtually everything else one says to the status of 'things one says.'"

Bending Chiasson a bit, this is an excellent way of

*thinking about the photograph's double-edged rela-
tionship to the actual. Considered in isolation, 'what
happened' is the province of photojournalism or the personal snapshot. The pictures at issue herein are different
in their construction: they are 'things one says,' which
nonetheless secondarily and massively benefit from the
credibility of 'what happened.'*

*Fortunately for us, Henry James happened to use the
term 'picture' when he wrote, "A story... has to choose
between being either an anecdote ['something that has
oddly happened to someone'] or a picture... I rejoice in
the anecdote, but I revel in the picture..."*

*Finally: according to Heidegger, "We are what we say
to one another."]* 34

34   There's something related to all this that Stevens
wrote in his "Adagia," and it brought me up short
when I first encountered it: "Most modern reproduc-
ers of life, even including the camera, really repudiate
it. We gulp down evil, choke at good."

    See, now that's the problem, stated in a different
and better way: what Greenberg gently characterized
as anecdotal or reportorial is for Stevens a straight-up
replication. Those are not the kinds of pictures I'm
talking about in this book, but still you see why the
general public—and even the photo-literate—often

The photograph, like any aesthetic object, is a new thing in the world. While it comprises the mind and the real, it is only *something you say*—'true' neither to self nor to not-self.

Perhaps this is a notion we are hard-wired to resist? "Helping deal with a world they do not understand, symbols are useful tools;" John Gray writes, "but humans have an inveterate tendency to think and act as if the world they have made from these symbols actually exists." 35

view photographs in this way: as mere imitations, formally (and thus emotionally) subordinate to the subject matter. Whether the problem lies with the photograph or the viewer, what is perceived in this case is merely the given, and, alas, not the possible.

35   Szarkowski, always a lively and amusing writer, is at his funniest on what this means for the viewers of photographs. Considering the work of Helen Levitt, he says: "Some might look at these photographs today and, recognizing the high art in them, wonder what has happened to the quality of common life. The question suggests that [her] pictures are an objective record of how things were in New York's neighborhoods in the 1940s. This is one possible explanation. Perhaps the children have forgotten how to pretend with style, and the women how to gossip and console,

With respect to photography, our engagement, to use Szarkowski's phrase, is with "pictures concerned not with how the world is constructed but with the more ambiguous question of what it looks like."

and the old how to oversee. Alternatively, perhaps the world that these pictures document never existed at all, except in the private vision of Helen Levitt, whose sense of the truth discovered those thin slices of fact that, laid together, create fantasy."

Or this classic bit from the essay in *William Eggleston's Guide:* "If a stranger sought out in good season the people and places described here they would probably seem clearly similar to their pictures, and the stranger would assume that the pictures mirrored real life. It would be marvelous if this were the case, if the place itself, and not merely the pictures, were the work of art. It would be marvelous to think that the ordinary, vernacular life in and around Memphis might be in its quality more sharply incised, formally clear, fictive, and mysteriously purposeful than it appears elsewhere, endowing the least pretentious of raw materials with ineffable dramatic possibilities. Unfortunately, the character of our skepticism makes this difficult to believe; we are accustomed to believing instead that the meaning in a work of art is due altogether to the imagination and legerdemain of the artist.

"It would indeed be marvelous... if the place itself, and not merely the pictures, were the work of art."

Description is
Composed of a sight indifferent to the eye.

It is an expectation, a desire,
A palm that rises up beyond the sea,

A little different from reality:
The difference that we make in what we see

And our memorials to that difference,
Sprinklings of bright particulars from the sky.

Description is revelation. It is not
The thing described, nor false facsimile.

It is an artificial thing that exists,
In its own seeming, plainly visible,

Yet not too closely the double of our lives,
Intenser than any actual life could be,

Thus the theory of description matters most.
It is the theory of the word for those

For whom the word is the making of the world,
The buzzing world and lisping firmament.

It is a world of words to the end of it,
In which nothing solid is its solid self.
—ws

This may sound like working with a camera means having one's cake (enjoying the full benefit of the real) and eating it (maintaining space for the unreal) too.

Perhaps it is the case that we get more than we deserve. As Wright Morris has noted: "Of all those who find more than they seek, the photographer is preeminent."

Which I take to mean: the photograph has the potential to be useful because it takes unique and effective advantage of the stuff of the not-self, while also manifesting the ineffable self. To crib from Stevens, we make use of the exact rock to discover our inexactness: the view which we desire endlessly.

Furthermore, real photographic greatness is achieved when form (*what is not*) is at least as important as subject matter (*what is*). The flipside of that coin: pictures are misread when subject matter is either over-emphasized or over-valued, when the given eclipses the possible.

This is because a photograph is the *articulation* of something, and not the mere portrayal of it. The latter is at best a list of one or several nouns (all external); the former is a set of relationships (also all external, but modeling the meeting of internal and external) that embrace verbs and prepositions and the like. 36

36   We confuse an interesting picture and a picture of something interesting. It should be easy to dismiss a photograph that seems to be simply pointing at some compelling thing; once the documentation is comprehended, the image is exhausted. Why look at it again?

Even in more well-balanced pictures, 'strong' subject matter can undermine the picture by overshadowing the correspondences within it. "A grandiose subject is not the assurance of a grandiose effect but,

most likely, of the opposite," says Stevens, and amen.
This, it seems to me, underlies the primary challenge
of portrait photographs. People are just too damned
fascinating on their own; way more often than not,
the presence of a human being (especially one looking
directly at the camera) overwhelms the picture.

"Once you insert a person into the work, he or
she becomes the protagonist and… that throws everything off," John Gossage once said in a conversation
with Lewis Baltz. "I want the viewer to be the protagonist." Baltz agreed: "I think this is one thing we have
in common: that the subject of the work is the person
looking at it. If you want to get a little more Zen
about it, the subject is necessary for the completion
of the work."

So there we go: for a picture to be interesting,
the viewer must be actively called on to complete it,
creating (ongoing) relationships between self and
photograph in a reverse parallel of the process of the
photographer creating relationships between self and
world—the maker assumes a kind of intimacy with
the viewer and exploits this confidence by giving us
work to do. The picture of an interesting thing, on the
other hand, is already concluded, its meaning hermet-
ically sealed within, and the viewer need do no more
than register this and move on. Adapting Stevens to

The camera enumerates the actual as does no other medium. It is the photographer's obligation to honor that power by exceeding it.

such a photograph: "While we are moved by it, we are moved as observers. We recognize it perfectly. We do not realize it. We understand it rather than participate in it." Participation must be ongoing; it is what is meant of the Supreme Fiction that "It must change."

Related, and going back to pictures of people, I'm often surprised by the observation that a portrait is 'more about the photographer than the person in the photograph.' Because 1) is it not clear that a photograph of a tree is also more about the maker than it is about the tree? And 2) it's *precisely the problem* of the portrait photograph when the opposite is the case, when the subject matter overpowers the picture. And then 3) it's a different and probably worse problem of 'central casting' when the picture is so obviously about the photographer that the person is denied all autonomy and merely fulfills the maker's notions of what that type of person (romantically downtrodden, more often than not) should look like.

And then there's the common estimation that the presence of the camera has an impact on the person in front thereof. Why yes, it does. Unless the subject is caught unawares, how could it be otherwise? An easel and pencils or paints, or a tape recorder or notebook, would have basically the same effect. Just as your presence *without any of these things* changes the behavior of any human being. (A sub-observation is

2. THE MOMENTARY /
   THE TRANSIENT

For the general viewer (and also for the sophisticated
one, in most cases), the photograph is synonymous
with its moment of exposure.

However much unsung work takes place both before
and after the shutter is released, a photograph feels
very quickly made. 37

> that the person being photographed is 'performative.'
> As we are all performative, even when alone ('signal-
> ing,' as the current science tells us), again, I do not
> see how this could be otherwise. What's interesting
> is the kind and degree of performance, and what the
> photographer makes with that—and then the subtle
> judgments we viewers make of all that.) Let this be
> baked into the very idea of a photographic portrait:
> the maker is, by definition, working with a camera
> and a person to make something called a 'picture' that
> is itself *not the depicted person*.

37   It also, of course, appears very *easily* made, and
       the next step is to say of any particular photograph
       that it could have been made by anyone. Szarkowski
       was writing before digital cameras, let alone smart
       phones, when he said: "In photography, as in belles
       lettres, we have reached the point of understanding
       that anyone can do it, and must now explore the

So quick—so fleeting—that it feels like experience itself. Like thinking.

[Wittgenstein wrote: "I look at an animal and am asked: 'What do you see?' I answer: 'A rabbit.' —I see a landscape; suddenly a rabbit runs past. I exclaim 'A rabbit!'

"Both things, both the report and the exclamation, are expressions of perception and of visual experience. But

more difficult fact that some do it better, and with better reason, than others."

The proliferation of images has been a real worry for a lot of folks in our world. The gist of the concern seems to be that if everyone has a camera all the time—and they're not afraid to use it and post the results—how are we to separate the good from the bad, and maybe also what does that even mean anymore? But I wonder: have poets ever been frightened by the wide availability of pencils? Much more recently, music seems to have survived and thrived as people who can't play instruments are able to create entire sonic landscapes.

Through all of this, we've been able to see through the clutter to those works of original perception and intelligence. And although we can easily ignore those who think that anyone could have made any photograph, I like how Szarkowski so forcefully gives the lie to all that in his consideration of a very plain and very *the exclamation is so in a different sense from the report: it is forced from us. —It is related to the experience as a cry is to pain.*

"But since it is the description of a perception, it can also be called the expression of thought. —If you are looking at the object, you need not think of it; but if you are having the visual experience expressed by the exclamation, you are also thinking of what you see.

"Hence the flashing of an aspect on us seems half visual experience, half thought."

This is what I'm getting at. Stevens says, "A poem is a pheasant." Same thing, much shorter.] 38

amazing picture by Henry Wessel: "It would be only half true to say that anyone could have made the picture, even aside from the fact that Wessel was probably the only one present when he made it. The basic point is that one would have had first to determine precisely what one meant by it (since the picture did not exist as a guide), and then consider it worth making. Granting these two conditions, almost anyone could have made Henry Wessel's picture."

38   But still, just to rein this in a bit, the photograph is ultimately a picture, and not itself a thought. Vendler

These revelations are not merely recounted, they are enacted. The photographs I admire most are thusly provisional: the impetus to the picture and the picture itself seem to have collapsed into one. Where the result is, in Chiasson's words, "a sense of the self as constituted by its immediacies."

writes that thinking "must enter somehow into the imaginative and linguistic fusion engaged in by the poem. While retaining its fierce intelligence, poetic thinking must not unbalance the poem in the direction of 'thought.' The image itself, as both the product of thought and the bearer of thought, becomes thought made visible." In her criticism, she hoped to "establish poets as people who are *always* thinking, who create texts that embody elaborate and finely precise (and essentially unending) meditation." I would argue the same for photographers.

Do you see that when this happens, it is form (the possible) that leads and subject matter (the given) that follows? Vasily Kandinsky wrote: "It is clear that the choice of object that is one of the elements in the harmony of form must be decided only by a corresponding vibration in the human soul."

But also: "It is the subject in poetry that releases the energy of the poet," as Stevens said.

I understand entirely why Valéry warns us not to "confuse the composition of a work of the mind, which is a finished thing, with the very life of the mind—which is a power of transformation always in action," but it's actually *something close to that very conflation* that I believe is the unique province of the photograph.

Cartier-Bresson says that the camera "questions and decides simultaneously." 39

And this comes through in the end result: "It is as if we follow the artist *as he is coming to a conclusion*," Thompson writes, "we take part in the critique along with him; we share in his thinking."

Blessedly, the photograph is not *precisely* like moment-to-moment experience. Like all aesthetic objects, it is made to defy transience.

[When alignment with life through poetry is achieved—once "I call you by name," says Stevens to his sensibility—"You will have stopped revolving except in crystal." This is an exceedingly appropriate metaphor for the products of the camera.]

39   Valéry himself said something remarkably similar: "The poet chooses among these [combinations of words], not the one which would express his 'thought' most exactly (that is the business of prose) and which would therefore repeat what he knows already, but the one which a thought by itself cannot produce, and which appears to him both strange and a stranger, a precious and unique solution to *a problem that is formulated only when it is solved.*" (emphasis mine)

Unlike any other aesthetic object, the photograph is a thing that embodies transience: it is an action *made of time* (its brief duration noted on the shutter setting) that results in a thing that *endures in time.* This peculiarity is one source of its unique power.

As Stephen Shore writes, "A photograph is static, but the world flows in time. As this flow is interrupted by the photograph, *a new meaning, a photographic meaning, is delineated.*" (emphasis mine, and this is super important for what I have to say from here on out)

We are overwhelmed with commentary on "photographic meaning." But shockingly little of it addresses what seems so clearly its greatest gift, which is that *photographic meaning is a comfort*: a "sudden rightness" as Stevens would say. 40

40   Why are so few people satisfied with (let alone comforted by) photographic meaning? A lot of folks seem to want to justify an affinity for photographs or photobooks by saying what they're 'like' or how they 'operate' in relation to other mediums.

Here's something I hear a lot: that photography is a language. I get that this is said admiringly, and probably it works on a meta level: one could think of 'fashion photography' or 'art photography' as having a semiotics. But my concern is the photograph, and to approach this entirely singular sort of picture as a language or a sign system is to misunderstand its essence.

Stevens wrote: "The words of things entangle and confuse. / The plum survives its poems."

Right. Because language is an abbreviation of the real, an abstraction in itself, the story or lyric is a second-level abstraction: a fiction constructed of many individual fictions. ("Every word was once a poem," said Emerson.) The fact that we're totally used to this doesn't keep writers from bemoaning it. Auden thought it "both the glory and the shame of poetry that its medium is not its private property, that a poet cannot invent his words," and rest assured there's plenty more where that came from.

Papageorge asserts that this observation "could

It is a relief, a momentary stay against the ceaseless ache of existence, and for me it is absolutely, 100% necessary.

Note, again, that photographic meaning is a *new* meaning: it is equivalent to neither its internal nor its external sources.

also be said of the photographer's relation to the things of the physical world: he cannot invent them," which is true but I think misses the point; the photographer of course does not (to her everlasting credit) fabricate the things in front of the camera, but she undeniably contrives *her relation* to those things; that's what the picture *is*. Auden's half-gripe is that he's forced to invent with that which is already an invention (with all its baked-in advantages and disadvantages).

What I'm getting at is that, among aesthetic objects, photographs are the closest thing we have to first-level abstractions; the camera denotes without itself connoting, and no talk of the signifier/signified is necessary: here there is nothing conventional or arbitrary—only what is indicated.

(Speaking of painters and sculptors, Gombrich is convincing in his assertion that "The artist, no less than the writer, needs a vocabulary before he can embark on a 'copy' of reality," and "that even to describe the visual world in images we need a developed system of schemata." Agreed. Human marks and gestures

To hijack Eliot: photographs are these fragments we have shored against our ruins. Just as any sense of wholeness in life is tentative and incomplete—fragmented—so are these pictures we stitch together to assuage our inadequacy.

> I cannot bring a world quite round,
> Although I patch it as I can.
> —ws

must start somewhere, building upon existing abstractions. But in the photograph, every house and every tree utterly resists our habitual generic schemes for what houses and trees look like. ("These are not things transformed," Stevens wrote, "Yet we are shaken by them as if they were.") The camera can't possibly rid the self of its chronic projections, but it does a superb job of thwarting them in the picture.)

Precisely the great thing about the camera is its ability to short-circuit language and existing representational models, and this gets at not just photographs but at personhood; as Joshua Rothman pointed out: "Heidegger… argued that our selfhood resides not in our language-based thoughts but in the interplay of our skills, habits, and moods. Who we are is defined more by our way of interacting with the world than by our beliefs." What is the camera other than an utterly singular way of interacting with the world? One that can help to clarify the selves of those who use it attentively.

And back on the level of the photograph: we're
just not in the business of subject-verb-direct object
(and to boot: such causative structures—which arise
from our grammar—lead us to misapprehend a world
that simply doesn't behave sequentially), and not even
really in photobooks.

Which gets us to the desire for 'narrative,' particularly in books. Here again we're denying a unique
advantage of our medium to satisfy a restrictive—
and ultimately unnecessary—objective that lies
outside of photography. Woolf says that "Life is not
susceptible perhaps to the treatment we give it when
we try to tell it;" she seems to be practically begging
for a camera with her almost impossible ambition
for the novel:

"Look within and life, it seems, is very far from
being 'like this.' Examine for a moment an ordinary
mind on an ordinary day. The mind receives a myriad
impressions—trivial, fantastic, evanescent, or engraved
with the sharpness of steel. From all sides they come,
an incessant shower of innumerable atoms; and as
they fall, as they shape themselves into the life of
Monday or Tuesday, the accent falls differently from

What else brings comfort? Knowing that other people feel the same way.

There is relief in the recognition that we are not so solitary as we suppose ourselves to be. That someone else managed to acquire a vantage that is somehow sufficient. That the longing which seems (and *is*) so

of old; the moment of importance came not here but there; so that, if a writer... could base his work upon his own feeling and not upon convention, there would be no plot, no comedy, no tragedy, no love interest or catastrophe in the accepted style.

"Let us record the atoms as they fall upon the mind in the order in which they fall, let us trace the pattern, however disconnected and incoherent in appearance, which each sight or incident scores upon the consciousness."

Replace 'atoms' with 'photons' and you almost literally have photography.

Now maybe you're thinking that what Woolf desires in the novel sounds a lot like poetry (which she pretty well achieved in *The Waves*) and that it would be nice to think of photographs similarly. Well, take a number, because everyone's doing it.

I'm never sure when a writer describes photographs as *poetic* if they mean 'dramatic' or 'narrative' (*ahem*) or 'lyric' poetry. They never seem to say, but I suppose they intend the lyric? In most cases, it's clear that they just like the pictures, and, alas, they can't personal is also a shared experience, in significant ways. Shared at the very least with the photographer who made something of it.

> You think your pain and your heartbreak are unprecedented in the history of the world, but then you read. It was books that taught me that the things that tormented me most were the very things that connected me with all the people who were alive, who had ever been alive.
>
> —JAMES BALDWIN (JB)

say *prosaic* because that has a (regrettable) pejorative connotation.

I'm not going to solve the question of what is and isn't poetry, but one thing is certain: in a lyric poem, the sound of the words is at least as important as (if not quite a bit more than) the sense thereof. (To be more specific, the sound is meant to make its own sense; this is true of anything 'literary.') "The 'something said' is important, but it is important for the poem only in so far as the saying of that particular something in a special way is a revelation of reality," Stevens wrote.

Because consideration of poetics adds contour to the relationship of form and subject matter in the photograph, it does seem less detrimental to talk about our medium in this way than it does when we invoke language or narrative. But if we go there, we must be precise in what we mean, in order to respect both the poem and the photograph.

So here's what it means: if a photograph is to be considered poetic, then its form must be of primary regard vis-à-vis its subject matter. In other words, the possible (the *how* or the *why* of the picture) is more important than the given (the *what*). This needn't imply a bright line between the poetic and the non-, but rather an approach for thinking about a range of photographs.

A practical example: the work of Robert Adams. He's got a bunch of books, and within each—and over the course of them—he is in clear and constant calibration between the outer and the inner. In almost pure terms of the latter, we have *Notes for an Overcast Day*. (Would one ever think of this book as information about leaves?) Nearby is *Listening to the River*, and here the sound is evidenced not only in the pictures themselves but in the humbly experiential sequences of from two to six photographs in any spread.

At the other end of the spectrum is *Turning Back*, in which the real-world issue of environmental degradation comes very close to overshadowing the maker's formal remove (as perhaps it must, given the urgency of its topic), and here's where I'd like to have

Jerry L. Thompson digs into something really crucial and slightly unnerving when he invokes privacy in relation to the maker's self: Photographs "give us matter for thinking because they combine a convincingly real image of the world with a measure of control resembling the shaping power we take as evidence of artistic vision... This mixed state of affairs, this marriage of the public and the private,

an agreeable word meaning 'prose-like.' In between— in *The New West* and *denver* and *What We Bought*— the hard Colorado light and especially the action of the squarish aspect ratios place more emphasis on the stuff of the picture, while the longer and looser and strangely darker pictures of *California* and *Los Angeles Spring* could be seen as speaking more to Adams's interior state.

See if all of this doesn't roughly comport with Yeats's observation that "We make out of the quarrel with others, rhetoric, but of the quarrel with ourselves, poetry." In any case, without definitively settling Adams into (ultimately unnecessary) categories, you can see that this model could be used for thinking about anyone's pictures. But to be clear: it can only be useful because the underlying nature of the poetic—the priority of sound over sense—relates specifically to the permutations of the possible and the given that constitute the photograph. Whereas my other point is that the character of language and

provokes thinking not only from those who look at photographs but also from some of us who make them." 41

Again: the correspondences (between external objects and events) that are fashioned into an aesthetic object can model our internal relationships of understanding, of knowledge. Of the private and the ineffable.

[If form-making is the essence of being human, the reverse is also true: we can experience the human

> of narrative (and of other mediums and related concepts) themselves do little to illuminate—and in fact come to deny—the unique virtues of photographic meaning.

41   Lewis Baltz writes that the value of photography is in "describing the surfaces of the phenomenal world in a manner unique to itself; hoping, at best, to contribute a precise, if necessarily limited, understanding of the objects and events in front of the lens, and *some insight into the mind behind it.*" (emphasis mine)

Or listen to Winogrand on seeing Evans: "That is the first time I was ever moved by photographs. I don't mean that I wanted to cry; I don't mean that by 'being moved.' It's the first time I was aware that photographs themselves could describe intelligence."

in aesthetic form. Which is strange and powerful; I don't know about you, but I can't *not* puzzle back to whatever it was in the maker (not biography, but rather the very jar on the nerves) that demanded the made. "Dickinson calls on us, as forensic Chemists of verse, to reconstruct from a small heap of Ashes—her poem—the self originally nourished and then consumed by the light of insight and the Fire of emotion," says Vendler.

Stevens wrote of "the thing that is incessantly overlooked: ...the presence of the determining personality," without which "no amount of other things matters much." Henry James called it the "question of the projected light of the individual strong temperament... something that proceeds from the contemplative mind itself, the very complexion of the mirror in which the material is reflected."

The first time I read David Foster Wallace in Harper's, I was fascinated and sort of creeped out because it felt just like my brain worked: disjointed, parenthetical, racing wildly ahead and then lagging behind, footnoting and sub-footnoting. And I do mean felt: the essays weren't at all descriptions of self (the topics were tennis and state fairs and cruise ships), but rather enactments *of self, on the page. The effect didn't arise from what he was saying; it was entirely a product of how he was saying it. (Authorial intent is of little consequence. Authorial consciousness is everything.)*

No other writer had managed to hit me that way before; not even close. The parts of me that felt too singular and weird and probably embarrassing now seemed much less so, and maybe even something to be prized. I had to read everything I could find by this guy, to immerse myself in his utterly individual meaning-making because it was illuminating and enlarging my own ability to make meaning of my self. And making me feel not so isolated in my mind.]

Some of the models made by other people will feel deeply familiar to us, so much so that we feel less alone. "In every work of genius we recognize our own rejected thoughts; they come back to us with a certain alienated majesty," says Emerson. We get a new and thrilling sense, "found within [our] world, another world, or nest of worlds; for the metamorphosis once seen, we divine that it does not stop."

This divining is a wondrous thing. Because it does not stop, we must now take it a step further: just as the thoughtful *viewing* of a photograph can help us to understand its maker, the conscientious *making* of photographs can help one to know—and even to create—one's self.

BEING A PHOTOGRAPHER

The limitations we sense in the photograph—of the actual and of time—are felt keenly by those who use a camera, in ways that are simply not realized by the painter or the poet or anyone else. Strangely, we can never seem to get enough of these particular limitations.

Photographers, like all artists, choose their medium because it allows them the most fully truthful expression of their vision. Other ways are relatively imprecise and incomplete.
—RA

To state the (maybe not always) obvious: when working with a camera, one cannot assemble the world to one's desire. "I still believe mainly in the opportunities afforded by acceptance," says Adams.

[If one can or does actively arrange (which is obviously possible, and often done), then the resulting object—however impactful—does not carry the kind of photographic meaning that I'm getting at here.

Applying Shore's formulation, the consequential delineations do not occur at the moment of making, but rather in the pre-exposure manipulation of the subject matter or the post-exposure alteration of the negative or file.

This is all totally fine, but it's important to point out that the pressure of neither the actual nor the transient plays a part in these kinds of photographs. And so they lie outside of my concern.]

Which brings us to decreation in its second sense: the purposeful restraint of our internally created projections upon the world to make space for the (non-created) givenness of things.

This aspect of decreation suggests a metaphysics *particular to the photographer,* with a resultant ethics for working with the camera.

> It is so beautiful here, if one just has a good & single eye without too many beams in it. And if one does have that eye, then it is beautiful everywhere.
>
> We are still a long way from that, however, since there are often beams in our eye that we know not of. Let us therefore ask that our eye may become single, for then we ourselves shall become wholly single.
>
> —VvG

> The more intensely one feels something that one likes the more one is willing for it to be what it is.
> —ws (and this could be read vice-versa)

> If you stand right fronting and face to face to a fact, you will see the sun glimmer on both its surfaces, as if it were a cimeter, and feel its sweet edge dividing you through the heart and marrow, and so you will happily conclude your mortal career. Be it life or death, we crave only reality.
> —HDT

I've mentioned Wallace Stevens's lifelong task of calibrating the distance between mind and world. Sometimes (and more often in his early career), this led to poems that projected desire onto the actual. At other times (and relatively more in his late work), Stevens allowed the real to push back against, and even dominate, the emanations of self.

Throw away the lights, the definitions,
And say of what you see in the dark
That it is this or that it is that,
But do not use the rotted names.

How should you walk in that space and know
Nothing of the madness of space,

Nothing of its jocular procreations?
Throw the lights away. Nothing must stand
Between you and the shapes you take
When the crust of shape has been destroyed.

Pearce categorizes the former poems as products of *transformation*, in which the poet is subjugating the real, and the latter as those of *decreation*, in which the poet is being subjugated by the real. "We find it easier to work through transformative mode than decreative mode," he writes. Poems of decreation "are not easily available to us because we must work through denial and doubt as a condition of achievement and certitude." 42

Either mode can succeed in poetry, as we "realize and celebrate the meaning that the poet, having confronted reality one way or the other, can give to the world."

42   If you're interested, transformative poems (according to Pearce, and I agree) include: "Sunday Morning," "Le Monocle de Mon Oncle," "The Emperor of Ice-Cream," and much of *Harmonium*.

Whereas the decreative poems are more like "The Snow Man," "Anecdote of the Jar," and on to "Notes Toward a Supreme Fiction," "Credences of Summer," and the great work of *The Auroras of Autumn* and *The Rock*.

Alas, photographers are not exactly poets. Because we cannot arrange the world to meet our projective whims, we lack significant access to the transformative mode.

[As previously mentioned, the determined maker can certainly skirt the limitations of working with the camera to contrive transformative pictures. But such documents necessarily deny the felt limitations of human contingency that underlie the unique kind of meaning inherent in the photograph. Is it not obvious that there can be no yearning for that which can be so easily manipulated?]

> Longing is the only magic of which we are capable.
> —EDGAR OLIVER (EO)

To be clear: decreation is not a normal everyday human function. The transformative is our default mode; it takes no effort at all to project the self onto the world.

> The state of mind of a photographer while creating is a blank... For those who would equate "blank" with a kind of static emptiness, I must explain that this is a special kind of blank. It is a very active state of mind really, a very receptive state of mind, ready

Achieving anything resembling the decreative state
is a chore, and revelations are fugitive. But worth the
effort.

Erase then, all mental activity from the blackboard
"reality." How stark the world looks. And for how
short a time it remains devoid of our meanings. The
symbol-mongering mind quickly intervenes between
blankness and self. But at least for a moment we've
started where Stevens does.

—SUSAN B. WESTON (SBW)

First let's admit that true decreation is impossible.
We lack any sort of direct ontological language that
would allow us to know things in their givenness.

Nietzsche was even more skeptical: "The 'thing-in-it-
self' nonsensical. If I remove all the relationships, all
the 'properties,' all the 'activities' of a thing, the thing
does not remain over; because thingness has only
been invented by us owing to the requirements of
logic." Stevens considered this also:

Yet the absence of the imagination had
Itself to be imagined.

Even if we did have an adequate means of expression, and could somehow evade our inventions, our

162

senses—rich and wonderful as they are—are severely empirically limited.

> ....we suspect our instruments. We have learned that we do not see directly, but mediately, and that we have no means of correcting these colored and distorting lenses which we are, or of computing the amount of their errors.
>
> —RWE

And so decreation is truly just a method, an active skill—a scrutinizing attitude with the goal of destabilizing one's established attitudes toward the world.

> The love which brings the right answer is an exercise of justice and realism and really *looking*... It is a *task* to come to see the world as it is.
>
> —IM

> For one day as I lent over a gate that led into a field, the rhythm stopped; the rhymes and the hummings, the nonsense and the poetry. A space was cleared in my mind. I saw through the thick leaves of habit. Leaning over the gate I regretted so much litter; so much unaccomplishment and separation...
>
> To see things without attachment, from the outside, and to realise their beauty in itself—how strange! And then the sense that a burden has been removed; pretence and make-believe and unreality are gone, and lightness has come with a kind of

Decreation also relates to time, in that it forces one to observe the current moment. Lewis Hyde notes that "unconscious automatic awareness engages only with the recognizable already known, that is to say, with things that match existing memory traces, those whose roots lie in the past, not the present, and the present is the only place where life is actually available."

So once again, we are considering the actual and the present.

And we see that a basic decreative mode is what the camera offers. In using this particular machine, one has no choice but to yield to the given and the now.

It's this surrender that is the great gift of photography, not only because the products of the camera
can be uniquely moving to viewers, but even more
so because of its beneficent effect on the maker. 43

Ultimately, it's about the acceptance of one's internal
limitations (as well as the external stuff: the things
and particularly the people of this world), and

43   As for the terms of our surrender—the subjugation of the transformative aspects of imagination
in favor of the real—the upside that Stevens saw
for the poet is even more evidently the case for the
photographer:
    "The poet finds that as between these two
sources: the imagination and reality, the imagination
is false, whatever else may be said of it, and reality
is true; and being concerned that poetry should be
a thing of vital and virile importance, he commits
himself to reality, which then becomes his inescapable
and ever-present difficulty and inamorata. In any
event, he has lost nothing; for the imagination, while
it might have led him to purities beyond definition,

an approach to life that corresponds with this acceptance (which is the topic of the next section).

Before we move on, though, there are practical—even technical; we use a machine, after all—matters of self-knowing and self-making for the photographer to weigh.

While we can't arrange the world with a camera, we have the ability to create significant associations between the things of the world and time *in the photograph*, and these purely pictorial correlations can help us to manifest and understand their ineffable counterparts of the within and the without.

never yet progressed except by particulars. Having gained the world, the imagination remains available to him in respect to all the particulars of the world. Instead of having lost anything, he has gained a sense of direction and a certainty of understanding. He has strengthened himself to resist the bogus. He has become like a man who can see what he wants to see and touch what he wants to touch. In all his poems with all their enchantments for the poet himself, there is the final enchantment that they are true. The significance of the poetic act then is that it is evidence. It is instance and illustration... Above all it is a new engagement with life."

The camera *is all about* creating relationships that are unreal (in that they never existed in the world) among things that are absolutely and recalcitrantly real. In fact, that's all it *can* do. 44

Again: although the photograph is the aesthetic object most obviously aligned to—and most achingly limited by—the actual, it is still an abstraction. It

44   Valéry is speaking of poems—but it seems also apposite to photographs, our "uncertain formations"— when he says: "...known objects and beings are in a way—if I may be forgiven the expression—*musical-ized*; they have become resonant to each other and as though tuned to our own sensibility.

"It appears and disappears capriciously, but man has done for it what he has done or tried to do for all precious and perishable things: he has sought and found the means to reconstruct this state at will, to recover it when he wishes, and finally to develop arti-ficially these natural products of his sensitive being. He has, in a way, been able to extract from nature and withdraw from the blind hurry of time these uncer-tain formations or constructions.

"So the poet's problem must be to *draw from this practical instrument* [language] *the means to realize an essentially nonpractical work.* As I have already said, his task is to create a world or an order of things, a system of relations unconnected with the practical order."

is always a fiction and must be scrupulously known and honored as such by its maker, out of respect both for the self and the not-self.

Szarkowski writes that the photographer had to learn that the factuality of pictures, "no matter how convincing and unarguable, was a different thing than the reality itself. Much of the reality was filtered out in the static little black and white image, and some of it was exhibited with an unnatural clarity, an exaggerated importance. The subject and the picture were not the same thing, although they would afterwards seem so. It was the photographer's problem to see not simply the reality before him but the still invisible picture, and make his choices in terms of the latter." 45

45   It is more difficult to evade

        That habit of wishing and to accept
            the structure

        Of things as the structure of ideas.

        Here again, Stevens could be writing specifically
    for the photographer, who must accept the uncooper-
    ative actual as the basis of aesthetic conceptualization.
    We see the unselfing demanded by the camera in the
    making of things, and moreover the defeat of wishful
    thinking—which is to say of solipsism—in life.

Yes: *choices* in terms of the picture. Which we should naturally regard as the *ethics* of the photograph, and of its maker. These are the practical manifestations of one's theoretical approach to the world (one's metaphysics).

Szarkowski and Shore have both written on the formal variables (and their expressions in the picture) through which the photographer knows the world and thus the self.

Szarkowksi speaks of: The Thing Itself, The Detail, The Frame, Time, and Vantage Point. It must be noted that with regard to The Thing Itself, he does not engage with the potential meaning of any particular subject matter, but rather with the givenness of all subject matter.

Writing more specifically for makers, Shore is a bit more technically instructive with his list: Flatness, Frame, Time, and Focus.

Shore could be speaking for both when he says that these choices "define the picture's depictive content and structure. They form the basis of the photographer's visual grammar... They are the means by which photographers express their sense of the world, give structure to their perceptions and articulation to their meanings."

The articulation of meaning, and not the mere identification of subject matter, is why photographs matter at all.

At risk of overstating the obvious: imagine turning ten photographers loose on a lone oak tree in a grassy field at the same time in consistent light. Why are the resulting pictures guaranteed to be so substantially different and (perhaps) variously interesting? Obviously not because of the subject matter, but rather because of the myriad formal choices—each with inherent limitations—of camera and lens and framing and exposure (and yes also because of decisions after that, but mainly because of actions in the moment) that have very little to do with subject matter, but which instead manifest an idiosyncratic sensibility as it jostles with the givenness of the actual. 46

46   "I saw and approached the hungry and desperate mother, as if drawn by a magnet. I do not remember how I explained my presence or my camera to her,

The point of the game is to know, love, and serve
sight, and the basic strategic problem is to find a
new kind of clarity within the prickly thickets of
unordered sensation.

—JSz

Photographers who come up with power never get
accused of imitating anyone else even though they
photograph the same broom, same street, same
portraits.

—MW

The mind of the photographer is known by its enunciations: the formal relationships it forges among the
things it frames.

An etymological detail that Kenneth Clark raises in
his discussion of landscape—*paradise* is the Persian
word meaning "a walled enclosure"—stands I think

but I do remember she asked me no questions. I
made five exposures, working closer and closer from
the same direction." These are the words of Dorothea
Lange, regarding the making of the photograph
known as *Migrant Mother*. The subject matter of this
picture is quite interesting on its own. But if mere
documentation was her goal, a single negative would
have been sufficient. Lange wanted a different thing
altogether: an interesting photograph; which is how
she arrived at an iconic one.

These enunciations are precisely delineated (both
happily and frustratingly) by the nature of the
machine and the materials. Which means that each
specific technical and physical choice carries great
weight of meaning in the final product.

*[The formal options and activities available to the
photographer are informed by both forgetting and
decreation, often in combination. Selections of camera
(aspect ratio, film size, lens and film plane movements),
lens (coverage, speed, sharpness), and film (negative or
transparency, color or black-and-white, ISO and grain)
are made over long periods of cultivated experimentation and judgment and abandonment.*

*Choices in the moment—framing, vantage point, and
exposure combinations of aperture and shutter speed—
are perhaps more obviously decreative in the sense of the
relationships we create and, within those relationships,
how much we project our selves or not. But then framing
is clearly restricted by the aspect ratio we've previously
chosen, and exposure decisions by type of lens, and so on.*

My point is not to be exhaustive about technical options (and several of my friends would laugh if I tried), but to insist that the formal choices that any one photographer makes—if there is to be any chance of aligning the interior world with the exterior—are complex and highly variable and at all times require the acutest care and attention to self and gear and world.

And what's more: these choices make *the photographer, both as artist and as person. Papageorge has written that Winogrand was inspired by Frank's use of the wide-angle lens and the way it shaped the world. "He started using a lens that could describe an even wider field of view; his pictures became more complex... Within three years he had found and mastered a photographic style, and with it,* a large part of himself*." (emphasis mine)]*

The photographic enterprise of experimenting with and exploiting all these variables as a way of creating imaginative correspondences is really just a specialized or concentrated version of the way in which all people know the world in moment-to-moment experience.

To harp on a theme: it's all about placing yourself
and your machine in various relationships to the
world in order to get at relationships between your
self and the world.

Using the camera must thus be seen as a method of
epistemological inquiry.

Ernst Cassirer tells us that "the term 'episteme' is ety-
mologically derived from a [Greek] root that means
firmness and stability." The photographer does yearn
always for secure footing. 47

47   I'd been stuck for a long time using the term
'medium' to categorize creative works: painting,
sculpture, video, dance, etc., whatever distinguishes
curatorial departments in museums. I'm grateful for

the way in which Thompson brought the word back round to making, and thus to knowing:

"By *medium* I intend to suggest a means of mediating a significant connection with the world. We say of a writer that language is his or her medium; we mean that this artist *finds his way* by using words. He may have an intuition or a feeling about things, but he works toward an understanding and expressed account of this intuition or feeling by using words.

"Similarly, photography can serve as a medium. Photographers use *things they see* and the *elements of seeing* instead of *words* and *grammar*. They use the act of photographing the world—the photographic encounter—as a means of finding their way or understanding the world. They arrive at understanding by photographing."

Paul Strand said that even after humans invented God, we were still curious. At first, art filled that excess speculative need, but eventually—and regrettably—science took over. For Strand, photography is a sort of technologically enabled reversion to an earlier state: "the first and only important contribution, thus far, of science to the arts." The camera, as a machine, "is a passive and an innocent party. The control of its mechanism and materials, the fineness and sensitivity of its accomplishments, are those of man. The new God shorn of its Godhead becomes an instrument of intuitive knowledge."

The camera can even be thought of as a component of the 'extended mind,' adopting the concept from the cognitive philosophers Andy Clark and David Chalmers. The classic example here is Scrabble tiles: the rearrangement of these inert things in the playing of the game should rightly be considered "not part of action; [but as] part of *thought*." Along these lines, Clark recounts

...the famous exchange between the Nobel Prize-winning physicist Richard Feynman and the historian Charles Weiner. Weiner, encountering with a historian's glee a batch of Feynman's original notes and sketches, remarked that the materials represented a "record of [Feynman's] day-to-day work." But instead of simply acknowledging this historic value, Feynman reacted with unexpected sharpness:

"I actually did the work on the paper," he said.

"Well," Weiner said, "the work was done in your head, but the record of it is still here."

"No, it's not a record, not really. It's working. You have to work on paper and this is paper. Okay?"

Feynman's suggestion is, at the very least, that the loop into the external medium was integral to his intellectual activity (the "working") itself. But I would like to go further and suggest that Feynman was actually thinking on the paper.

Similarly, we are thinking *with* and *through* the

camera. This gets back to something I mentioned earlier: real in-the-moment thinking (and not the illustration of previous thoughts) happens when the impetus to the picture and the picture itself are one and the same. It's not about what the photographer *knows*, but what she can *make*. Clark and Chalmers:

> In these cases, the human organism is linked with an external entity in a two-way interaction, creating a coupled system that can be seen as a cognitive system in its own right. All the components in the system play an active causal role, and they jointly govern behavior in the same sort of way that cognition usually does... The relevant external features are active, playing a crucial role in the here-and-now. Because they are coupled with the human organism, they have a direct impact on the organism and on its behavior. In these cases, the relevant parts of the world are in the loop, not dangling at the other end of a long causal chain.
>
> The external features in a coupled system play an ineliminable role—if we retain internal structure but change the external features, behavior may change completely. The external features here are just as causally relevant as typical internal features of the brain.

Think specifically about those modifications of external features. Consider how changing cameras,

or even just switching lenses, alters your behavior:
how your mind (and also the weight of your body,
your moving feet) meets the world in a way that
is at least meaningfully, and perhaps profoundly,
different.

Notice that everything I have said, or tried to say,
happened in relation to what we call the External
World, what we call Our Body, and what we call
Our Mind, and requires a kind of vague collaboration
between these three great powers. 48, 49
—pv

48   See how Valéry teased out the corporeal as a
       third element—not quite self and not quite world?
       With respect to the physical, let's borrow and apply
       another concept from Andy Clark: embodied cogni-
       tion. Above all else in using a camera, you are placing
       your self—both mind and body—in a specific rela-
       tion to the world. "You must be on the alert with the
       brain, the eye, the heart, and have a suppleness of
       body," as Cartier-Bresson said.
           In the *New Yorker* article that introduced me to

If the point wasn't already clear: Choices of aspect ratio or lens coverage or film type are not just things that impact how your prints look on the wall or in a book. They are the very structure of your mind when it meets the world with a camera.

all this, Larissa MacFarquhar writes that Clark "came to believe that if you were going to figure out how intelligence worked you had always to remember the particular tasks for which it had evolved in the first place: running away from predators and toward mates and food. A mind's first task, in other words, was to control a body. The idea of pure thought was biologically incoherent: cognition was always embodied.

"The line between action and thought was more blurry than it seemed. A creature didn't think in order to move: it just moved, and by moving it discovered the world that then formed the content of its thoughts."

To provide some context, Clark in his own writing quotes Esther Thelen: "The contemporary notion of embodied cognition stands in contrast to the prevailing cognitivist stance which sees the mind as a device to manipulate symbols and is thus concerned with the formal rules and processes by which the symbols appropriately represent the world."

Now of course, neither of these people is writing about the state of contemporary photography, but I think one can easily draw parallels to photographs

[Formal] decisions resonate with the clarity of the photographer's attention. They conform to the photographer's mental organization—the visual gestalt—of the picture... It is a complex, ongoing, spontaneous interaction of observation, understanding, imagination, and intention.

—STEPHEN SHORE (SS)

that manifest in-the-moment thinking in the world and those which manipulate symbols that merely represent the world.

Clark quotes John Haugeland's "benchmark assertion that: If we are to understand mind as the locus of intelligence, we cannot follow Descartes in regarding it as separable in principle from the body and the world... Mind, therefore, is not incidentally but intimately embodied and intimately embedded in its world."

Yes. Photography is often spoken of as the walker's medium, which is certainly true, but it's way more than that. Think of the bodily contortions you'll make, the disregard for creaky knees and ankles, the search for things to stand or climb on, all because you know innately not only that your position in the world is your world, but also crucially that that position — for the photographer only — *is what you can make of your world.*

And those are just the active maneuverings. Consider the passive: how your body sags when you're sad, how your shoulders clench when you're anxious, or how well and tall you stride when delighted. Just as,

Technical choices must be made with great care for your pictures, but even more importantly with the utmost respect for your separate self and your intelligence and the contents of your heart (which are—or should be—basically *the same thing as your photographs*).

quoth Goethe, "A man sees in the world what he carries in his heart," the emotions that color your view of the world also directly influence the way you employ your camera.

"Training may bring the photographer's eye to a kind of secular awareness," Papageorge says, "but the body, which moves with it, also forms and sees with its own singular pressure. Athletes know this, and probably anyone else who seriously practices."

"Whatever things I perceive with my entire man, those let me record, and it will be poetry," Thoreau wrote.

49   As I said just above, the photographer locates herself in a certain position vis-à-vis the world. You might say this could be equally so for the painter or draftsman who works *en plein air*. But here's the thing: unlike those artists unbound by the actual, it is the very placement of the photographer's body that is fundamentally determinative (along with the formal controls of the camera—which we can now see clearly as expressors of the self—adjusted in response to physical location) of the content of

Photographic seeing is an intentional way of continually discovering and rediscovering integrations of self and not-self. In a photograph, the mind of the maker is fleetingly apprehended.

> It is putting one's head, one's eye, and one's heart on the same axis… It is a way of shouting, of freeing oneself, not of proving or asserting one's originality.
> —HENRI CARTIER-BRESSON (HC-B)

> For it is the pressure of the values that creates the intensity of the work, and to assume otherwise is to have no comprehension of how art actually happens.
> —PETER SCHJELDAHL (PS)

her eventual print. It is one's physical relation to the world in the making of the exposure that governs the relationships made manifest in the picture. Again: these formal associations are the bearers of the photograph's significance.

In other words, with a camera: making = meaning.

To repeat: your aesthetics are your ethics. 50

There is one point at which the moral sense and
the artistic sense lie very near together; that is in
the light of the very obvious truth that the deepest
quality of a work of art will always be the quality of
the mind of the producer.

—HJ

50   Szarkowski says of Atget that his "personal
perceptions seem to achieve perfect identity with
objective fact. There is in his work no sense of the
artist triumphing over intractable, antagonistic
life; nor, in the best work, any sense of the poetic
impulse being defeated by the lumpen materiality
of the real world."
        There are two interrelated claims here about
how the gauging of self and not-self has a direct
impact on the picture (or rather, as I've tried to
show, that these calibrations *are* the picture).
        The first point is easy enough to grasp: Atget
never permitted his projections to have undue
transformative power over the real. In other words,
his work is decreative in nature. The second is interesting because of the implication that such an
approach could, at least in some of Atget's work,
be *unsuccessful*—resulting in pictures thwarted by
the actual. It's important to consider this because,
although I've emphasized a preference for the decreative, there of course must be limits.
        The chaos of the actual is gently described by

I've always been amazed that no photography writer (that I know of) has made much use of the eye/I homophone that's practically a cliché in poetry.

The camera as eye = the camera as self.

Szarkowski as 'lumpen,' but recall that Stevens saw it as much more malign; for him the imagination is "a violence from within that protects us from a violence without… pressing back against the pressure of reality."

In his finest pictures, Atget allows his internal poetry—his self—to emanate only precisely enough to meet the frenzied forces of the external. This is why one so often hears that his photographs have an unmistakable grace.

And here again, in different words, my thesis: working productively with the camera demands an achieved equilibrium of mind and world. Although this hard-won stability gains a measure of permanence in the photograph, it remains of course ultimately evanescent in real life. Like grace, it is fleeting; but it impresses upon the maker, enriching her person. It is a comfort.

"It seems, in the last analysis, to have something to do with our self-preservation," Stevens wrote, "and that, no doubt, is why the expression of it, the sound of its words, helps us to live our lives."

So: don't take this lightly, and *do not fuck this up*.

IV

THE FINAL YES

"I have discovered camera is both a way of life and not enough to live by," Minor White wrote.

Same here, but I doubt that *any* vocation, taken alone, could ever really suffice. My more modest—and yet entirely grand—claim is that lessons learned from working with the camera can be meaningfully extrapolated to the whole of life, and much to our benefit.

Before we get to that, take note (you probably already did) of the definite article that White left out of his revelation. The grammar is awkward, but it's characteristic of his generous mindset to reposition the concrete noun as something abstract like dignity, or love. This is not such a leap: when we think of our favored machine as embodied, as an epistemological tool, we see that it is no longer simply 'the' camera. It is part of us; an aspect of self.

The limitations of camera uniquely echo the limitations of the human. In no other medium is one both so frustrated and so rewarded by the real: by our utter powerlessness to impress upon it but also by our power to make something lasting and useful of it by creating consequential relationships within the photograph, thus bringing significant form to bear on the existential conundrum.

> After the final no there comes a yes
> And on that yes the future world depends.
> No was the night. Yes is this present sun.
> If the rejected things, the things denied,
> Slid over the western cataract, yet one,
> One only, one thing that was firm, even
> No greater than a cricket's horn, no more
> Than a thought to be rehearsed all day, a speech
> Of the self that must sustain itself on speech,
> One thing remaining, infallible, would be
> Enough.
> —ws

In embracing the constraints of photography as a facet of self, one acquires, by analogy, a practical method for more fully realizing one's personhood.

Thoreau could easily have been writing about those who make use of the camera: "The scenery, when it is truly seen, reacts on the life of the seer. How to live. How to get the most life. How to extract its honey from the flower of the world."

My contention is that one's aesthetics both engender and dignify one's ethical approach to existence. This is "our affair," says Stevens, "which is the affair // Of the possible: seemings that are to be, / Seemings that it is possible may be."

The basis of all this lies in the supreme teaching of the camera: humility in the face of the actual and of unrelenting time: the absolute thusness of all that is not the self.

Paradoxically, the humbling of one's self to the non-negotiables of our existence (recognizing them, and working—creating and decreating—maximally within them) results in a freedom of real consequence.

As we make peace with our constraints, we are able (in fact, we are called) to pronounce the triumph of that act.

HUMILITY

I've written a lot about the actual with respect to the photograph—how it's the source of the document's enigmatic power, despite (or rather because

of) the profound manner in which the camera con-
strains the making.

But now let's expand on the beneficial aspect of this delimiting: what the experience of working with the camera might mean for the bigger struggle—how it might help the photographer to recognize that which *is* enough to live by.

Stevens writes: "[Art must] mediate for us a reality not ourselves and this is what the poet does and the supreme virtue here is humility, for the humble are they that move about the world with the lure of the real in their hearts."

See how this flips the whole thing on its head? The obstinate becomes the object of desire for those willing to unself before it. The path for the photographer is something like this: the long-term practice of working with the recalcitrant real gradually engenders a genuine respect for the meaningless, impersonal, transient, actual world *on its own terms,* and this reverence quite naturally grows into longing for (and, wonderfully, consolation by) that which previously resisted (and which still resists) easy assimilation.

[Note that Stevens placed the longing for the real in our hearts, not in our heads. I think there's a rational aspect to it all, as well... In any case, recognize yet again how uncannily it seems he could've been writing specifically about photographers.]

The desire that Stevens evokes is for Being itself —a Being that is staggeringly unlikely.

In a perfect universe, we would not exist.

> According to the dictates of Einsteinian relativity and the baffling laws of quantum theory, equal numbers of particles and their opposites, antiparticles, should have been created in the Big Bang that set the cosmos in motion. But when matter and antimatter meet, they annihilate each other, producing pure energy. Therefore, the universe should be empty of matter.
>
> That didn't happen, quite. Of the original population of protons and electrons in the universe, roughly only one particle in a billion survived the first few seconds of creation. That was enough to populate the skies with stars, planets and us.
>
> —DENNIS OVERBYE (DO)

It now appears that we owe it all—the earth and the heavens and Lucinda Williams—to neutrinos, which seem to be "the flimsiest excuse on which to base our existence... famed for their ability to waft through ordinary matter like ghosts through a wall. They are so light that they have yet to be reliably weighed," as Overbye writes.

Being is thus richly, marvelously improbable. And slight. Contingency is the condition not just of our limited human lives, but of the entirety of the universe. 51

51   Which makes the cosmos and us folks all of a piece, if one thinks along the lines (as I do) of Marilynne Robinson:
"[The capacity for abstract thought] must have arisen out of the transformations potential in that first particle and realized over time, consistently with these potentialities. Then, if this is the case, there is a profound, intrinsic relationship among all forms of Being.
"By implication, Being is addressed to the mind as the mind is addressed to Being. Both should be thought of as emergent. Being infused with its roaring history and on its way to somewhere or something, but, given the difference between its time and ours, as if paused to tolerate our contemplation of it. And then the mind reaching after it. To call it Deus absconditus would not be wholly wrong, since it is both hidden and manifest, elusive and radically sustaining. I suppose I always find myself writing theologically

This understanding, Iris Murdoch thinks, should take us down a notch or two: "The acceptance of death is an acceptance of our own nothingness which is an automatic spur to our concern with what is not ourselves," she writes, and for her this concern for the not-self equates with humility, which is "a rare virtue and an unfashionable one and one which is often hard to discern. Only rarely does one meet somebody in whom it positively shines, in whom one apprehends with amazement the absence of the anxious avaricious tentacles of the self... The humble man, because he sees himself as nothing, can see other things as they are."

because only theology supports an ultimate coherency that can embrace equally the true, the tentative, and the flawed, as reality itself embraces them—which is only to say that we, our erring kind, are as intrinsic a part of reality as mice and moonlight."

What function has the shutter other than to pause Being long enough for us to contemplate it, and thus also to expose the entirety of the breach between the timetables of the human and the cosmic? It's that very disparity that leads me to differ from Robinson: there's no fundamental coherence, and nothing that could support such, but I do wholeheartedly embrace the tentative and the flawed. As does the camera.

Again, decreation: the achieved mode of the person who accepts the sharp limitations of everyday existence. The mode also of the photographer, whose machine (as extended mind) is so similarly constrained by the conditional.

For Murdoch, this approach is an essential strength: "Humility is not a peculiar habit of self-effacement, rather like having an inaudible voice, it is selfless respect for reality and one of the most difficult and central of all virtues."

Flannery O'Connor would agree: "We hear a great deal about humility being required to lower oneself, but it requires an equal humility and a real love of the truth to raise oneself and by hard labor to acquire higher standards." 52

52   I agree with O'Connor that acquiring higher standards in life is possible if we are unsparing in our assessments of the things we make. What she says of the writer is even truer of the photographer:
"The fact is that the materials of the fiction writer are the humblest. Fiction is about everything human and we are made out of dust, and if you scorn getting yourself dusty, then you shouldn't try to write fiction. It's not a grand enough job for you.

Achingly, she concludes: "Art requires a delicate adjustment of the outer and inner worlds in such a way that, without changing their nature, they can be seen through each other. To know oneself is to know one's region. It is also, paradoxically, a form of exile from that world... and to know oneself is, above all, to know what one lacks. It is to measure oneself against Truth, and not the other way around. The first product of self-knowledge is humility."

We are confronted here again with the brokenness: the lack, the exile that is inseparable from knowledge of the self. That indeed *is* the self.

> "Conrad said that his aim as a fiction writer was to render the highest possible justice to the visible universe. That sounds very grand, but it is really very humble. It means that he subjected himself at all times to the limitations that reality imposed.
> "What the fiction writer will discover, if he discovers anything at all, is that he himself cannot move or mold reality in the interests of abstract truth. The writer learns, perhaps more quickly than the reader, to be humble in the face of *what-is*. *What-is* is all he has to do with; the concrete is his medium; and he will realize eventually that fiction can transcend its limitations only by staying within them." (emphasis mine)

Objective, external truth (admittedly unattainable) is the standard by which we are to be redeemed, and not by what's inside. Any attempt at wholeness will require humility in the face of the real.

Not incidentally, we need this humility, this practice of unselfing, to even find common ground with other human beings: "The corporeal world exists as the common denominator of the incorporeal worlds of its inhabitants," Stevens wrote.

This is all tied together: the candid and scrutinizing search for integration of mind and world, through the making of aesthetic objects, cultivates integrity in and of the person.

["The self, the place where we live, is a place of illusion," Murdoch writes. "Goodness is connected with the attempt to see the unself, to see and to respond to the real world in the light of a virtuous consciousness. This is the non-metaphysical meaning of the

idea of transcendence to which philosophers have so constantly resorted in their explanation of goodness. 'Good is a transcendent reality' means that virtue is the attempt to pierce the veil of selfish consciousness and join the world as it really is. It is an empirical fact about human nature that this attempt cannot be entirely successful.

"Goodness is connected with the acceptance of real death and real chance and real transience and only against the background of this acceptance, which is psychologically so difficult, can we understand the full extent of what virtue is like. [The humble person] sees the pointlessness of virtue and its unique value and the endless extent of its demand... The only thing which is of real importance is the ability to see it all clearly and respond to it justly which is inseparable from virtue."] 53

Murdoch again: "We discover value in our ability to forget self, to be realistic, to perceive justly... The authority of morals is the authority of truth, that

53   Recall Papageorge's reference to "that more footed joy and grief found near any clear sighting of the world." The idea of those emotions being associated with virtue brings us nearer where we want to be.

is of reality... We can see it as natural to the particular kind of creatures that we are that love should be inseparable from justice, and clear vision from respect for the real."

[*Clear vision is indeed the goal, and humility in our hearts and minds must be our guide. While the valuation of Being is exclusively human, the whole thing will go on merrily enough without us.*]

We realize Being in our engagement with what we call the Thusness or Givenness of things (always hinted at by the indicative 'thisness' of the photograph); that which, as Murdoch writes, "resists absorption into the selfish dream life of the consciousness."

> The path of things is silent. Will they suffer a speaker to go with them? A spy they will not suffer; a lover, a poet, is the transcendency of their own nature—him they will suffer. The condition of true naming, on the poet's part, is his resigning himself to the divine aura which breathes through forms, and accompanying that givenness.
>
> —RWE

A spy will not be suffered by the Given—but a poet, perhaps. "We want to be the poets of our lives, and first of all in the smallest and most commonplace matters," Nietzsche wrote.

Again, and alas, we have no ontological language to know things directly, and no ability to get out of our own way even if we did. So, no spying, and certainly no transcendent meeting of self and not-self; rather we must inch gradually and modestly toward

Being, like an asymptote forever approaching but never reaching its curve.

One wanted, she thought, dipping her brush deliberately, to be on a level with ordinary experience, to feel simply that's a chair, that's a table, and yet at the same time, it's a miracle, it's an ecstasy.

Let me sit here forever with bare things, this coffee-cup, this knife, this fork, things in themselves, myself being myself.

—VW

The walls are pale violet. The floor—is red tiles.
The wood of the bed and the chairs is the yellow of
    fresh butter, the sheet and the pillows very light
    lime green.
The blanket scarlet.
The window green.
The washstand orange, the basin blue.
The doors lilac.
And that's all—nothing of any consequence in this
    shuttered room.

—VvG

It is desire, set deep in the eye,
Behind all actual seeing, in the actual scene,
In the street, in a room, on a carpet or a wall,

Always in emptiness that would be filled
—WS

Amen to the small and the commonplace, the things of no consequence. "Wherever you turn your eyes the world can shine like transfiguration," Robinson writes. "You don't have to bring a thing to it except a little willingness to see. Only, who could have the courage to see it?" 54

54   Vuillard asked: "Why is it that familiar places are where mind and sensibility find what's genuinely new? This newness is always necessary to life, to consciousness." As we've seen, flux is incessant, both inside and out: "We stand in the tumult of a festival," Stevens wrote. But when we engage with the familiar, we take a bit of control over one of the variables—by calming the external down somewhat—which affords us space to observe the calibrations of the mind, to discern "the movement of the self in the rock."

The camera calls upon us not only to be empiricists (to see the world as objectively as we can) but also to recognize that our objectivity necessarily manifests some level of idiosyncratic subjectivity—and then to be empiricists of that secondary realization as well.

To ruthlessly observe and manage and cultivate this process is our task.

This is exhilarating because what we find inside

Well, of course, the author herself has shown the courage, time and again. And she has identified at least a couple conspirators: "The most persistent and fruitful tradition of American literature from Emily Dickinson to Wallace Stevens is the meditation on the given, the inexhaustible ordinary."

Coincidentally (but not really, when you think about it), Dan Chiasson has said that "Both Dickinson and Stevens used the minute changes of familiar landscapes and preferred times of day to make extraordinary claims for the mind's powers of transfiguration."55

will invariably be the genuinely new (the "internal difference, / Where the Meanings are" wrote Dickinson), whereas a new exterior scene alone can only be superficially new: novel as subject matter, but not as content. (Ezra Pound, by the way, never meant for us to go out and find previously unknown shit to talk about.) And, notably, Vuillard understands that this is bigger than art—that the ability to gauge the machinations of the self is essential to the vitality of our mental existence, and to the habitability of our world.

55   If we are to put great stock in the powers of the mind, then something must be said here about the comic. I didn't like it at all when I first heard Stevens's work described that way, but only because I wasn't

That's the whole deal, right? Laying claim to the powers of the self to create meaning where none otherwise exists, and understanding that, counter-intuitively, these powers are even more astonishing when harnessed to and constrained by the actual.

aware of the proper usage of the term; I should've been, because as Riddel suggests: Our transfigurations of the world are "dangerous to be indulged unless accompanied by a critical sense of how one's view of the world mocks one's limitations. The comic is the gesture of the human, offering a dramatic way of projecting the little vices of human egocentrism into a form which might free one from those vices." Making peace with the self's inability to ever truly come to grips with the not-self (while also recognizing mind as the only source for any sort of meaning in the world) seems to require—at least now and then—a comic stance.

Contrasting Stevens with Whitman—and this linguistically elegant distinction seems vitally important to me—Riddel says that "Notes Toward A Supreme Fiction" gives us a "comic, not a cosmic 'I,' the act of discovery, not ecstasy or vision... that release of emotion which man earns when he probes and discovers his world, his place in it, and its place in him."

The comic in this sense is essential to anyone who works with an interior bent, because such self-scrutiny is the only bulwark against self-indulgence. Pearce spoke of Dickinson's "steady concern with herself as being, for good and ill, at the center of

In my experience, this realization affords one a great deal of freedom.

her world. It is not a matter of egotism, but rather of a humble, tragic, pathetic, even humorous realization of limitations. The sense of limitation, realized as sharply as it is, is her greatest spiritual strength and forces her poems into their triumphant egocentrism."

"We are at bottom grave and serious human beings—really, more weights than human beings," Nietzsche wrote; and so "At times we need a rest from ourselves by looking upon, by looking *down* upon, ourselves and, from an artistic distance, laughing *over* ourselves or weeping *over* ourselves. We must discover the *hero* no less than the fool in our passion for knowledge; we must occasionally find pleasure in our folly, or we cannot continue to find pleasure in our wisdom."

FREEDOM

Here are some words from a Miracle Legion song that have guided me often over the years. I can find no official lyric sheet, so I've transcribed the lines in the way it sounds to me that Mark Mulcahy (the lyricist) sings them:

> There's no complaints
> That's how it is
> When
> You
> Are
> Free

We can't be rid of the ache of incompleteness, and honestly we wouldn't really ever want to be, but what we *can* do is manage and shape our short-term reactions to our predicament, along with our longer-term responses to it in the things we make.

> See what a life the gods have given us, set round with pain and pleasure. It is too strange for sorrow; it is too strange for joy.
> —HDT

That response cannot be merely grievance.

Everything I've said so far about the camera—
regarding its limitations and possibilities, and how
closely those match the limitations and possibilities
of self—should lead us naturally to the conclusion that working with this particular machine is a
weirdly and improbably effective way to turn chaotic experience into meaningful response—in other
words, to learn to just get along in the world. 56

William McEwan once asked Robert Adams: "With
all of the pictures and all of the books, what are you
trying to accomplish in your life in photography?"
Adams replied: "I suppose to learn not to complain."

To reprise a theme: Using a camera is all about
making bodily and mechanical choices to create
formal relationships between external things (the

56   A conclusion that was already in your heart and in
your head without need for this book or for anything
anyone else could ever say anyway.

picture) that model relationships between the internal and the external (the self).

The ability to choose meaningfully has long underpinned ideas of freedom.

Existence is a continuous confrontation with emergencies, competing desires, situations in which choices must be made. The ultimate meaning of existence is not an a priori given but one's ultimate commitment, the choice not of this or that course of action, but of a "mode of existence" within which all more particular choices may be determined.

This freedom of choice is itself the most basic of values, what makes a man a *human being* or an *existent individual*, and the recognition and use of this freedom is far more important than the object of choice. 57
—ROBERT SOLOMON (RS)

57   There are other thoughts on human freedom that are directly related to the aesthetic object; they're worth a little detour here. The basis of this thinking is Kant's differentiation between a thing that is purpose-

In engaging the question "what should I do?" we are also engaging the question "who should I be?" and there is no final answer to that question. This is our spiritual freedom.

My point is not to provide criteria for the difficult decisions regarding life and death, but to elucidate why their difficulty is an essential feature of leading a free, spiritual life. Existential anxiety is at work in every form of spiritual life, since it opens us to the question of what we *ought* to do with our time. Moreover, the anxious relation to finitude is not even ideally to be overcome.

ful and one that is purposive. The former—a hammer or a chair, for example—is an object with a practical use. The latter, in Paul Fry's words, "has its own inner purpose, which is not a purpose that has any bearing necessarily on anything else. It has, as one might say, an internal coherence. It has a dynamism of parts that is strictly with reference to its own existence. It is a form."

In other words, it engenders its own authority. Which, it must be admitted, is also to say that the purposive is not good for much. As I've mentioned before, it's not information about anything external to it; it can't relate to us any helpful or useful data; the poet "nothing affirms, and therefore never lieth," wrote Sir Philip Sidney.

In more other words, those of Oscar Wilde: "All art is quite useless."

Don't be fooled by the flippancy, because it disguises a profound insight into not only the autonomy

Our lives are of ultimate worth not because we are immortal or destined to do good, but because we are capable of leading our lives which always comes with the risk of doing harm or failing in our pursuits. These risks cannot and should not be eliminated, since they are part of what it means to lead a free life.
—MARTIN HÄGGLUND, MH

of the aesthetic object, but also the freedom of us persons. Fry explains, "Wilde is pointing out that art is uniquely useless; it appeals to no merely appetitive or exaltedly rational form of subjective interest [the appetitive and the rational mapping to Kant's "Understanding" and "Reason," both of which are entirely purposeful], hence we have no instrumental use for it. We can distance ourselves from our subjective wants and needs and likes and dislikes, and we can coexist with art in a happy and constructive way that is good both for us and the work of art, because if we recognize that there are things in the world which have intrinsic value and importance and what we call beauty, and yet are not the things that we covet or wish to banish, we recognize in ourselves the capacity for disinterestedness, and at the same time we allow the work of art to be free from our designs on it. We thereby recognize in ourselves an attribute, freedom, that is the cornerstone of many systems of value.

"To realize that we don't have to take an instrumental interest in things in order to realize that they are self-sufficient and valuable shows us something

But choosing is never easy. Because the distinct self exists solely *in the act of making choices.* 58

crucially important about ourselves. Wilde's suggestion, but I think also Kant's suggestion before him, is important for our recognition of our own value as independent moral agents. Disinterestedness entails the realization that freedom is possible not just for me but for those things in which I have no instrumental interest. What's implicit then in this view of art and of human judgment is that... it's a way of recognizing that in addition to all our other attributes, some of them wonderful, we are also free, autonomous."

And so the useless is useful beyond measure.

58   The existentialist philosophers valued highly the ability to choose, but underlying that was something even more important—the nihilating power of mind and the resulting Nothingness of consciousness. Which sounds pretty heavy, but it all lines up with the centrality of the imagination and the space it creates: 1) our ability to imaginatively transform the actual (to see possibilities among which to make choices) is also necessarily the capacity to negate it; and 2) since the products of our imagination—our forms—are utterly unbound by the actual, our consciousness lies outside of causal determination; mind is thus a 'Nothingness' because if it were 'something,' it would be part of the normal chain of worldly events, and consequently constricted by those events.

A reminder: the formal relationships we create, the result of myriad choices made in life and in art, are fictions.

"Admitting that our lives are shaped by fictions may give a kind of freedom—possibly the only kind that human beings can attain," Gray writes.

(Put aside the certainty that determinism is anyway just a bug in our language, and go with this—it's a solid backup plan.)

Which is all just to say that human consciousness is free.

It should not, however, be thought of as untethered. Our subjectivity needs objects about which to be subjective. Consciousness is reliant upon the actual, without which it would not exist. And Sartre digs into something crucial for us when he asserts (in Solomon's words) that "consciousness is absolutely nothing apart from its consciousness of objects, and that objects 'present themselves' as independent and 'fulfilled' or 'complete' in-themselves while consciousness (properly viewed) always presents itself as dependent, as 'unfulfilled,' as 'incomplete.'"

We see here again in different terms the mismatch

I happily admit this, and I also assert that a decreative (in both senses) approach—honed by working with the camera—can support self-determination in a fabricated world.

> The prologues are over. It is a question, now,
> Of final belief. So, say that final belief
> Must be in a fiction. It is time to choose.
> —ws

between *what is* and *what is not*, and the source of the fundamental lack that is selfhood. We are forever frustrated by our insufficiency (and resentful of a world that is oblivious to desire). This is the price we pay for the indeterminacy that is also our freedom.

I've been emphasizing something along these lines for the last couple-hundred pages: the unique combination of contingency and agency that is the essence of working with the camera. When I showed this book as a work-in-progress to some friends, I got some mild pushback on the title—on the linking of camera to death. I replied that I just meant (wordily) that 'To photograph is to learn how to reconcile the limitations of life,' but what I came to understand (less passively, but still not pithily) was that 'To photograph is to manifest one's freedom.'

To be sure, the painter and the poet have more 'freedom' in the objects they make; they can nihilate at will. With the camera, however, we are tethered to the things of the world, which remain "independent

With respect to decreative forgetting: the constant
cultivation and limning of our innumerable selves
is an essential—perhaps the ultimate—activity of
mind.

And further: as we encounter and comprehend per-
spectives different from our own, we're less likely
to value our own solipsistic projections so highly,
or to see them as so central to self. Such modesty

and fulfilled" even as we create formal relationships
(aka significance) between those things in the
photograph.
    "Our freedom does not destroy our situation, but
gears itself to it," Sartre writes, and for this equation of
human agency with form-making, I claim him for our
medium.
    This is precisely why the camera is singular
(superior) in getting at the ineffable: it exposes (and,
in the photograph, tentatively resolves) the inherent
lack that defines the self; it does this by honoring the
world in its thusness. In other words, our machine
is decreative in nature while simultaneously allowing
the photographer to manifest the ache of his incompleteness and the formal will—the freedom—to
choose among relationships and possibilities, and
thus to effect human meaning.

    FORM = POSSIBILITY = FREEDOM = SELF

is surely an asset in a decreative approach to the things of the world. 59

59 Stevens wrote:

> Freedom is like a man who kills himself
> Each night, an incessant butcher, whose
>   knife
> Grows sharp in blood.

Note here that the blade is not dulled but rather made all the more effective by its endless and pitiless use. Perhaps it is with this weapon that we take arms against our sea of troubles? Hamlet's conundrum was whether to passively bear "The heart-ache and the thousand natural shocks / That flesh is heir to" or to take potentially drastic action: "by opposing" his troubles thus to "end them."

Stevens is clear: there is no end. The friction of the real is never to be overcome; freedom is a bloody ceaseless mess. If death is for Hamlet the only potential way out of the ache (whether or not one reads him as seriously considering ending his own life), then Stevens exceeds Shakespeare by invoking a decreative suicide *that is actually freedom in this life.* This is the potency of self gained by an active observation of the controllable and the uncontrollable, and a brutal scrutiny and tending thereof.

Observation, scrutiny, tending—all within the unforgiving limitations of the real: the tasks specifically of the person who would work with the camera.

Decreation in the second sense—the active curtailing of the projections of self—is equally integral to an earned autonomy.

Ethical progress is urged by our particular vocation because our machine does not mislead. (The photograph—that is another matter altogether.)

The camera will not indulge our every desire; as a tool for thwarting solipsism, it is unmatched.

What it does offer is something better and far stranger, something akin to grace: the peculiar ability to reconcile the profound constraints of self—by modeling them as disciplined relationships within the photograph.

216

The camera's unique limitations (and attendant possibilities) can inform our ethics, specifically because they so uncannily embody our human constraints.

We come to understand that our time spent working with the camera—a time of constant and deliberate formal calibration—can instruct the chaotic and improvised form-making of our everyday lives. This process fosters a ceaseless self-critique that is indispensable to achieving a freedom of personhood.

So: our concern now is not just the vital integrity of the fiction within the photograph, but also the very same writ large: the efficacy of camera in determining what can be perpetually affirmed in one's existence.

"We can be agents of life and not just patients of it," says Pearson. Again, Montaigne's take:

> Cicero says that philosophizing is nothing other
> than getting ready to die. That is because study and
> contemplation draw our souls somewhat outside our
> selves, keeping them occupied away from the body, a
> state which both resembles death and which forms a
> kind of apprenticeship for it; or perhaps because all
> the wisdom and argument in the world eventually

comes down to one conclusion; which is to teach us not to be afraid of dying.

All that you live, you have stolen from life, you live at her expense. Your life's continual task is to build your death.

Just as Montaigne sets us to an ongoing duty, Nietzsche says "Become who you are" and not merely "Be who you are."

AFFIRMATION

"When Jesus on the cross declares *consummatum est*, [Peter] Sloterdijk says that we ought to see this as a victor's cry, equivalent to that of a Greek athlete winning a race or a wrestling match," Adam Kirsch writes. "The phrase should be translated, he argues, not as a passive 'it is finished' but as 'Made it!' or 'Mission Accomplished!' For the conquest of death is the ultimate goal of all spiritual training, and the great founders—Jesus, Buddha, Socrates—are those who won the championship by dying on their own terms." 60

60   There's a very late Stevens poem called "The Planet on the Table" in which, in just five stanzas, the poet

Now of course, I haven't been aiming at anything 'spiritual'—I find the secular entirely sufficient—and yet a sort of religious language does inform much of the discourse around our work. "The point of the poem is that there must be in the world about us things that solace us quite as fully as any heavenly visitation could," Stevens wrote. Which is natural enough, seeing that making sense of our unfathomable transience in this world is of primary concern to pretty much all folks, whether one perceives meaning

examines the worth of his lifelong vocation—what he did with his scant time on this earth—and finds that "Ariel was glad he had written his poems."

I'm glad that he (Ariel = Wally) was glad. But the thing that really slays is what he does in the last two stanzas to extend such fulfilment to any maker, based on the significance of made things. Firstly, he tells us that worthiness lies not in the permanence of the poem or the picture: "It was not important that they survive." Rather:

What mattered was that they should bear
Some lineament or character,

Some affluence, if only half-perceived,
In the poverty of their words,
Of the planet of which they were part.

and purpose as external constants or as temporary internal constructions.

If it's true that the universe consists of atoms and void and nothing else, then everything that exists—the sun and the moon, mother and the flag, Beethoven's string quartets and da Vinci's decomposing flesh—is made of the elementary particles of nature in fervent and constant motion, colliding and combining with one another in an inexhaustibly abundant variety of form and substance. No afterlife, no divine retribution or reward, nothing other than a vast turmoil of creation

Everything here depends on the three progressive nouns—all aspects of mind and world—that the poem (read: photograph) should manifest. A 'lineament' is a visible feature of a thing, in a pretty-close-to-'objective' sense—something anyone might notice without need of personal embellishment. There's also a dictionary definition having to do with geology wherein the lineament is not an actual feature itself (such as a hidden fault line), but rather a mark on the land that reveals such a feature.

This subtlety leads us quite naturally to 'character,' a word more clearly imbued with human projection—a subjective weighing or valuation of that which underlies the observed. And then: jackpot: 'affluence,' because that's what I'm after: a surplus of meaning, riches inexplicably extracted by the aesthetic object from the nothingness of raw experience. For Henry James, this is the "sublime economy of art, which and destruction. Plants and animals become the stuff of human beings, the stuff of human beings food for fish. Men die not because they are sick but because they are alive.

—LEWIS LAPHAM (LL)

"Death is a constant reminder that in being there is potential unbeing," writes Riddel. "Our sense of the opposite of our being is formed out of the images of our being." He goes on, quoting Stevens: "Creator of itself, the self is the ultimate creator, creating

rescues, which saves, and hoards and 'banks.'... thus making up for us, desperate spendthrifts that we naturally are, the most princely of incomes."

Earlier—in relation to those occasions when the self does more than just forge a mutual pact with the actual (which, let's face it, is way more than enough most of the time) to summon that surfeit which is the aesthetic object (which, let's also face it, is pretty much the same overflow that we suffer as *love*)—I used the word 'profligacy.' There is indeed a wastefulness, a royal extravagance, that is inevitable when poesis demands to become poem.

This is because, as Stevens reminds us, we are doomed to failure on all fronts. The treasures of experience are never fully perceived; our instruments just won't allow it. And what's more: the things we make—even the greatest of them—are similarly destitute; words (and pictures) are unavoidably not only the knowledge of death, but the way—the mythology—by which one can accept it. In poetry one realizes not the 'end but the way / To the end.'"

Let this sink in a little: *our sense of death is constructed of the things we make from life.* This is really just an extension—a profound one, to be sure—of what I've been arguing all along: that we manifest our epiphanies (those momentary accords between the internal and the external, and time) in aesthetic objects, which are created sets of relationships between entirely external things.

Here is the ultimate argument for the usefulness to humans (the ethics) of the aesthetic object: that significant form (as beauty) can help to prepare its audience (and its maker) for non-being.

poor imitations of the evanescent agreements of mind and world that engender them.

And so here we make our peace: an abundance of meaning—which is precisely the usefulness of the poem or photograph (or of love) to human beings— lies in neither the strict recording of the world nor any exact report of the maker's self. And anyway, such chronicles would be merely things 'about;' our aim must instead be for constructing heretofore unknown things *of the planet of which they are a part.*

All poetic form, however newfangled, is necessarily metaphoric, a substitution of figurative for literal, of life for death.

—HB

By relinquishing technique he gained something else, a carelessness that allows the world to appear unfettered by how we happen to conceive of it. Van Gogh tried to commit himself to the world but couldn't do it, he tried to commit himself to painting but couldn't do it, therefore he rose above them both and committed himself to death; only then did the world and painting become possible for him. For the entire force of these paintings, all their manic light and singular power of penetration, which makes them appear as though the celestial were suffusing the earthly and lifting it up, is contingent on the look he casts upon it really being his very last.

—KOK

And to die is different from what any one supposed, and luckier.

—WW

It all comes down to this: you can give in to the cosmic dread, or you can make something useful that affirms being while still recognizing every bit of pain and difficulty. (The photograph must, since it necessarily embraces the actual, also manifest its poverty: the inability of the maker to ever bridge the gap between *what is* and *what is not*. It's not about 'truth,' but about what can be confirmed as sufficient.)

> The challenge for artists is just as it is for everyone: to face facts and somehow come up with a yes, to try for alchemy. No wonder the instances of artistic success are costly and rare and impure. And deeply loved. And utterly out of the reach of most journalists.
> —RA

Moreover, as a result of the "difficultest rigor" of this ethic—to use Stevens's phrase—the photographer knows that in such recognition lies the source of all human value in the face of a meaningless universe. "It is wholly an inner light, that... / Searches a possible for its possibleness."

Working with camera sanctifies the basic fiction of life; it is a freedom.

> ...being is deemed as holy enough to justify even a monstrous amount of suffering.
> —FN

> [Rilke wanted art to be a] cessation of desire; a place where our inner emptiness stops generating that need for things which mutilates the world and turns it into badly handled objects, where it becomes instead a pure, active, becalmed absence.
> —RH

"The passion for yes distinguishes Stevens from the existential dilemma," Riddel writes. "It's his retention of the imagination and thus the will to act joyfully in the face of absurdity."

The importance of joy cannot be overstated.

> Poetry is a health.
> —WS

> ...the *great health*—that one does not merely have but also acquires continually, and must acquire because one gives it up again and again, and must give it up.
> —FN

Trilling asserts that the "faculty of not having to make up one's mind about everything depends upon the sense of one's personal identity and is the sign of personal identity."

The sense of one's identity, and how one manifests that sense, is nothing less than an ethics.

> I would believe only in a god who could dance.
> —FN

> Well there's another dance
> All you gotta do is say yes.
> —BRUCE SPRINGSTEEN (BSp)

Have you ever said Yes to a single joy? O my friends,
then you said Yes to all woe. All things are entangled,
ensnared, enamored; if ever you wanted one thing
twice, if ever you said, 'You please me, happiness!
Abide, moment!' then you wanted all back. All anew,
all eternally, all entangled, ensnared, enamored—oh,
then you loved the world. Eternal ones, love it
eternally and evermore; and to woe too, you say: go,
but return! For all joy wants—eternity.

—FN

*["In later writings Nietzsche clarifies and refines what
it means to say 'yes' to life: it doesn't mean that one
says yes to everything and it doesn't exclude the 'no,'"
Pearson writes, "Our task is to be equal to everything
that happens in life, the great and small, the highest and
lowest. As he appreciated, there is something sublime in
this (something in the realm of the unknown)."]*

For the eternal tendencies of all toward happiness
make the only point of sane philosophy.

—WW

As Goethe said, this sort of love "does not dominate; it cultivates."

Love takes off the masks we fear we cannot live without and know we cannot live within. I use the word
"love" here not merely in the personal sense but as a
state of being, or a state of grace—not in the infantile

226

American sense of being made happy but in the tough
and universal sense of quest and daring and growth.
—JB

It is good to go on believing that everything is
more miraculous than one can ever begin to understand, for that is the truth; it is good to remain
sensitive and humble and tender-hearted even
though one may have to hide one's feelings, as is
often necessary.
—VvG

Do you see how, viewed in this way, love—otherwise
the most 'subjective' of emotions; in every love song
ever, reason is obliterated by passion—has a quality
approaching objectivity? That it supports an ethics?

Love that never attempted to clutch its object,
but, like the love which mathematicians bear their
symbols, or poets their phrases, was meant to be
spread over the world and become part of the
human gain.
—VW

"While you love, that which is innate in you becomes
malleable; so love shapes you," says Martin Amis.
Here again, an expansionary take on an idea previously entertained: that the made changes the maker.
But Amis isn't really talking about making; I'll take

liberty with his comment to assert that an objective attitude—a decreative approach to all that's not the self, which requires a hard-earned love for the recalcitrant real—alters you, and (if you're lucky) it can have a snowball effect.

Which really shouldn't be so hard to countenance, because how could the wholly internal (solipsistic) self be able to change without continual friction from the actual? How would it know itself to even be a present and ongoing self?

Gesang ist Dasein, singing is being, or song is reality, the moment when the pure activity of being consciously alive is sufficient to itself... Singing is being. It creates our presence.
—RH

Note the present tense. Creating our presence—our self—is a ceaseless undertaking, a making. And not a made thing. Or at least not once and for all; Frank

Kermode lauds Stevens's "determination to regard no armistice in the 'war between mind and sky' as a final treaty."

> What is life? — Life — that is: continually shedding something that wants to die... Constantly being a murderer
> (FN)

> We have made too much of life. A journal of life is rarely a journal of happiness.
> —WS

As I was thinking about this book, and then outlining it, and even as I was writing the first three sections, I had it in my head all along that any argument for learning how to die must naturally end with some concept of peace, an offering of a path to tranquility or serenity.

And I *have* made the case for harmony, insofar as it might be available to us. But an equilibrium of self and not-self can never be permanently achieved. It can only be faithfully tended—created and decreated—and in this work there can be no rest. As Montaigne said: "Your life's continual task is to build your death."

So frenzy it is (stormy, reflected, bestowed). *What is* and *what is not* locked in a joyous no-holds-barred duel to the death.

"Instead of trying to achieve a final peace of mind," Martin Hägglund writes, "we should own the existential anxiety of our freedom. If we had no anxiety about what to do with our time, we would not be able to discriminate between which activities are worthy and unworthy of who we take ourselves to be."

That's really all we can ever do: try to figure out how to be of use, to ourselves and others, within our limitations, by continuously choosing well between the worthy and the not.

This is our ethics. This is the gift of camera.

> It is possible, possible, possible. It must
> Be possible.
> —ws

For my family. I have all the love I could ever ache.

Of counsel:
Jenia Fridlyand, George Weld, John Kilbane, Raymond Meeks,
Brad Zellar, Terri Weifenbach, Charlie Simokaitis, Andrew
Bruah, Cheryl Van Hooven

Thank you:
Tricia Gabriel, RAL, Mary Frey, J Carrier, Nelson Chan, Carl
Wooley, John Gossage, Alec Soth, David Campany, Christian
Patterson, Adam Meeks, Nathan Pearce, Ron Jude, Edgar Oliver,
Jesse Lenz, Asako Oono, Jack O'Brien, Sneddon family, German
family, Mom & Dad (always, forever)

Coördination:
Jacques Marlow, León Muñoz Santini, Andrea García Flores

Mike Slack edited and designed this book. His generosity and
patience are beyond measure; I am grateful and indebted.

To photograph is to learn how to die: an essay with digressions
© 2022 Tim Carpenter for the text, except where noted
© 2022 The Ice Plant for this edition

Distributed by Artbook/D.A.P.
Printed in Italy by Grafiche Veneziane
ISBN 979-8-9857330-0-6 (sixth printing)

 The Ice Plant • PO Box 29247, Los Angeles, CA 90029

ABBREVIATIONS & CITED WORKS

AC   ANNE CARSON: *Autobiography of Red; Decreation;*
            "Variations on the Right to Remain Silent"

ACa   ALBERT CAMUS: *The Crisis of Man*

ACD   ARTHUR C. DANTO: *The Transfiguration of the*
            Commonplace

AM   AGNES MARTIN: *Agnes Martin*

BSp   BRUCE SPRINGSTEEN: *Tunnel of Love*

CW   CHRISTIAN WIMAN: *Ambition and Survival: Becoming*
            a Poet

DC   DAN CHIASSON: *One Kind of Everything: Poem and*
            Person in Contemporary America

DFW   DAVID FOSTER WALLACE: *Oblivion; Infinite Jest; A*
            Supposedly Fun Thing I'll Never Do Again; Consider
            the Lobster; Both Flesh and Not

DO   DENNIS OVERBYE: "The Neutrino Trappers"

DT   DONNA TARTT: *The Goldfinch*

EB   ELIZABETH BISHOP: *Poems, Prose, and Letters*

EC   ERNST CASSIRER: *An Essay on Man: An Introduction to*
            a Philosophy of Human Culture

EG   ERNST GOMBRICH: *Art and Illusion*

EO   EDGAR OLIVER: *In the Park*

FN   FRIEDRICH NIETZSCHE: *The Gay Science; Human, All*
            Too Human; Ecce Homo

FO'C   FLANNERY O'CONNOR: *The Complete Stories; Mysteries*
            and Manners

GF   GUSTAVE FLAUBERT: *Selected Letters*

HB   HAROLD BLOOM: *How to Read and Why; Take Arms*
            Against a Sea of Troubles: The Power of the Reader's
            Mind Over a Universe of Death

HC-B   HENRI CARTIER-BRESSON: *The Mind's Eye: Writings on*
            Photography and Photographers

HDT   HENRY DAVID THOREAU: *The Journal 1837-1861*

HF   HENRI FOCILLON: *La peinture au XIXe et XXe siècles*
HJ   HENRY JAMES: *The Wings of the Dove; Theory of Fiction*
HV   HELEN VENDLER: *Poets Thinking; Words Chosen Out of Desire*
IM   IRIS MURDOCH: "The sovereignty of good over other concepts"
JB   JAMES BALDWIN: *Collected Essays*
JG   JOHN GRAY: *Straw Dogs: Thoughts on Humans and Other Animals*
JNR JOSEPH N. RIDDEL: *The Clairvoyant Eye*
JSz JOHN SZARKOWSKI: *Mirrors and Windows: American Photography since 1960; The Photographer's Eye; Looking at Photographs*
KOK Karl Ove Knausgård: *So Much Longing in So Little Space: The Art of Edvard Munch*
LH   LEWIS HYDE: *A Primer for Forgetting: Getting Past the Past*
LL   LEWIS LAPHAM: "Memento Mori"
LT   LIONEL TRILLING: *The Liberal Imagination; The Opposing Self: Nine Essays in Criticism*
MB   MARIE BOROFF: *Language and the Poet*
MH   MARTIN HÄGGLUND: *This Life: Secular Faith and Spiritual Freedom*
MM   MARK MULCAHY: *Love's the Only Thing that Shuts Me Up*
MR   MARILYNNE ROBINSON: *Housekeeping; Gilead; When I Was a Child I Read Books; The Givenness of Things; What Are We Doing Here?*
MS   MARK STRAND: *The Weather of Words: Poetic Invention*
MW   MINOR WHITE: *Aperture Magazine Anthology: The Minor White Years*
PB   PIERRE BONNARD: *Letters Between Friends*
PÉ   PAUL ÉLUARD: *Quelques-uns des mots qui jusqu'ici m'étaient mystérieusement interdits*
PF   PAUL FRY: *Theory of Literature*

PS   PETER SCHJELDAHL: *The hydrogen jukebox*
PSt   PAUL STRAND: "Photography and the New God"
PV   PAUL VALÉRY: *The Art of Poetry*
RA   ROBERT ADAMS: *Beauty in Photography; Why People
        Photograph; Along Some Rivers; Art Can Help*
RE   RALPH ELLISON: "The Art of Fiction"
RH   ROBERT HASS: "Looking for Rilke"
RQ   RAYMOND QUENEAU: *For an Ars Poetica*
RMR   RAINER MARIA RILKE: *Letters on Cézanne*
RS   ROBERT SOLOMON: *Existentialism*
RWE   RALPH WALDO EMERSON: *Essays & Lectures*
SdB   SIMONE DE BEAUVOIR: *The Ethics of Ambiguity*
SS   STEPHEN SHORE: *The Nature of Photographs*
STC   SAMUEL TAYLOR COLERIDGE: *Complete Works*
SW   SIMONE WEIL: *Selected Essays*
TBB   THOMAS B. BYERS: *What I cannot say: Self, word, and
        world in Whitman, Stevens, and Merwin*
TP   TOD PAPAGEORGE: *Core Curriculum*
TSE   T.S. ELIOT: *Selected Essays*
VL   VERNON LEE: *The Psychology of an Art Writer*
VN   VLADIMIR NABOKOV: *Lectures on Literature*
VvG   VINCENT VAN GOGH: *A Life in Letters*
VW   VIRGINIA WOOLF: *The Waves; To the Lighthouse; Selected
        Essays*
VWi   VICTORIA WILLIAMS: *Loose; Swing the Statue!*
WHG   WILLIAM H. GASS: *Omensetter's Luck; In the Heart of
        the Heart of the Country; Finding a Form: Essays*
WM   WRIGHT MORRIS: *Time Pieces*
WP   WALTER PATER: *The Renaissance*
WS   WALLACE STEVENS: *Collected Poetry & Prose*
WW   WALT WHITMAN: *Poetry & Prose*

ISAIAH BERLIN: *The Roots of Romanticism*
LEWIS BALTZ: *Texts*

Christopher Beha: "Winning the Peace"

Wendell Berry: *Essays 1993-2017*

Andy Clark: *Supersizing the Mind: Embodiment, Action, and Cognitive Extension*

Emily Dickinson: *The Complete Poems*

Robert Frank: "A Statement"

John Gossage & Lewis Baltz: "A Conversation"

Clement Greenberg: "Four Photographers"

Larissa MacFarquhar: "The Mind-Expanding Ideas of Andy Clark"

Vasily Kandinsky: *Concerning the Spiritual in Art*

Adam Kirsch: "Against Cynicism"

Archibald MacLeish: *Poetry and Experience*

Miracle Legion: *Me and Mr. Ray*

Michel de Montaigne: *The Essays*

Siddhartha Mukherjee: "Runs in the Family"

Roy Harvey Pearce: *The Continuity of American Poetry*

Keith Ansell Pearson: *A Companion to Nietzsche*

George Saunders: *A Swim in a Pond in the Rain: In Which Four Russians Give a Master Class on Writing, Reading, and Life*

Sufjan Stevens: *Seven Swans; Illinois; Carrie & Lowell*

Jerry L. Thompson: *Truth and Photography*

Édouard Vuillard: *The Intimate Poetry of Everyday Life*

Wilco: *Being There; Summerteeth; Yankee Hotel Foxtrot; Ode to Joy*

Ludwig Wittgenstein: *Tractatus Logico-Philosophicus; Philosophical Investigations*

W.B. Yeats: *Essays 1931 to 1936*